The Economic Effects of Disarmament

The aim of this book is to show the current impact of defence expenditure in the United Kingdom, and to provide a guide to the problems likely to be met when changing to a non-defence economy. The issues covered include:
How would disarmament affect the United Kingdom economy?

Which industries depend on defence spending?

In which parts of the country is employment on defence work greatest?

How could spending on defence be replaced?

What effects could disarmament have on consumers' incomes, the social services, aid to developing countries, investment?

The
Economic
Effects
of
Disarmament

by The Economist Intelligence Unit
sponsored by the United World Trust

London
The Economist Intelligence Unit

Toronto
University of Toronto Press

Published by
The Economist Intelligence Unit Ltd.
5 Bury Street, London SW1

in North America
University of Toronto Press
Toronto, Canada
Reprinted 2017
ISBN 978-1-4875-9827-3 (paper)

Acknowledgements

The United World Trust would like to record its grateful thanks to all those companies, trade unions, charitable trusts and foundations and other organisations and individuals who have helped in financing this study.

The Economist Intelligence Unit wishes to thank officials of the Ministry of Defence and other government departments and also the large number of persons in industry throughout the country who completed the questionnaire and, in many cases, provided additional information and comments at subsequent interviews.

Without the assistance of all these individuals and organisations this survey would not have been possible.

Preface

This survey, to assess the economic consequences of disarmament in the United Kingdom, was commissioned by the United World Trust for education and research in February, 1961. It has two objectives:

1. to ascertain the extent and character of the economic resources at present employed by the current total defence budget of the United Kingdom government.

2. to consider in the light of this information a number of alternative policies for the re-employment of economic resources which would be released in the event of disarmament in the United Kingdom.

In carrying out this survey it was the aim of The Economist Intelligence Unit, and the wish of the United World Trust, to make it as factual and objective as possible. It is an attempt to show the current impact of defence expenditure on the United Kingdom economy and, by doing so, to indicate the possibilities that would be open and the problems that would have to be faced in the economic sphere if disarmament were to occur.

The report falls into two distinct parts; the first and larger of the two deals with the current impact of defence expenditure on the United Kingdom economy, and the second with the alternative uses to which the released resources might be put in the event of disarmament. It is essential to follow this pattern, since it is only after the impact of defence expenditure has been determined that any valid assessment is possible of the resources likely to become available if disarmament were to occur. Moreover, in the current political and economic situation it would undoubtedly be the policy of the government of the day to keep any industrial dislocation and unemployment arising from the ending of defence expenditure to a minimum, and this would limit the alternative uses which could be made of the defence revenue.

There are at present many competing claims on the economy which cannot be satisfied fully, and the removal of the need for defence expenditure would provide considerable scope for current and new civil projects—both in the public and the private sector. In the first instance, however, the need to match demands with the resources released will clearly act as a brake on the transfer from defence to civilian expenditure. For example, an increase in school, hospital and road building— each a project for which a good case could be made—could be met to only a very limited extent, if at all, by the labour and equipment released from the aircraft and electronics industries which currently receive a high proportion of the defence expenditure which goes to industry. In addition, the process of absorbing personnel of the armed services into civilian jobs will also take time and, in some instances, will involve lengthy and expensive retraining schemes if the best use is to be made of the men and women concerned.

Once the impact of defence expenditure on the economy has been assessed, it is necessary to determine the type of disarmament which is likely to occur—for the effects of partial disarmament would be significantly different in kind from those of total and complete disarmament. The assumption that has been made is that complete disarmament will occur and that it will be carried out by all the countries of the world. In the present circumstances, despite the possibility that some measure of control over nuclear weapons might be agreed upon before general disarmament, this seems to be the most useful assumption to adopt. It is interesting to note in this context, for example, that the Acting Secretary General of the United Nations, U Thant, in his preface to a report by the United Nations Economic and Social Council on 'Economic and Social Consequences of Disarmament' said that:

> 'In dealing with its economic and social consequences the experts have adopted the assumption that disarmament, once agreed upon, would proceed rapidly and would be general and complete'.

However, in the event of disarmament—certainly in the light of the current views of the western countries—it must be assumed that an inspection, and possibly an international armed force, would be maintained by the United Nations. Estimates of the probable running costs of such a force vary widely, and the capital expenditure required is thought by some experts to be so high that it would involve a greater outlay than the total of current national defence budgets. For this survey the possible capital costs have been ignored, and it has been assumed that the running costs of such a force would cost the U.K. approximately 5 per cent of its current defence budget. If national contributions are made on the same basis as the present payments to the United Nations, this implies a total international expenditure on the United Nations' force of about £1,120 million a year.

Before this survey was started permission was obtained from the Ministry of Defence to ask for information from individual companies by means of a questionnaire, and in a number of instances further details were obtained at interviews with the companies concerned. The responsibility for the conclusions reached and the presentation of the information obtained, however, is entirely that of The Economist Intelligence Unit Limited.

Owing to delays it was not possible to start the survey until September, 1961, and the research was mainly carried out between October, 1961 and March, 1962. Although much of the available statistical information covers the financial year 1961–62 as a whole and the employment figures relate to end-May, 1961, the conclusions reached in respect of particular industries refer to the situation as it was between those two dates.

September, 1962

THE REGIONAL
DISTRIBUTION OF
DEFENCE EMPLOYMENT
AND UNEMPLOYMENT
AT MAY 1961

EACH SYMBOL
REPRESENTS 10,000
WORKERS

EMPLOYED ON
DEFENCE CONTRACTS

UNEMPLOYED

SCOTLAND

NORTHERN

NORTHERN
IRELAND

E. & W. RIDINGS

N.W.

N. MIDLANDS

MIDLANDS

WALES

EASTERN AND SOUTHERN

S.W.

LONDON
AND S.E.

Contents

PART ONE

THE ECONOMIC EFFECTS OF

DEFENCE EXPENDITURE ON THE UNITED KINGDOM

1. *Defence and the Economy*

Chapter 1

The Level of Defence Expenditure

THE CURRENT LEVEL OF DEFENCE EXPENDITURE IN THE UNITED KINGDOM

The Statement on Defence, 1962—the annual White Paper which sets out the government's defence policy—estimates the cost of the defence programme in the financial year 1961–62 at £1,655·60 million,[1] and this is expected to rise to £1,721·06 million in 1962–63 (excluding the additional cost of the recent pay award to the Services, estimated at £14 million in 1962–63). In addition, a further £19·37 million is to be provided by the Civil Departments for home defence against £18·61 million in 1961–62. Of total estimated government expenditure for the financial year 1962–63 of £6,364 million, some £1,740·4 million or 27·1 per cent will be accounted for by defence. In the year 1961–62 the proportion was also 27·1 per cent after taking the Supplementary Estimates into account.

It is also estimated in the Statement on Defence, 1962, that the defence budget will amount to some 7 per cent of the gross national product. Moreover, the Statement, which is sub-titled 'The Next Five Years', gives a clear indication that expenditure will be maintained at about this proportion in future years, as can be seen from the following extract.

> '12. Our task here, the difficulty of which should not be under-estimated, is not to cut defence expenditure but to contain it. Although it is our present aim to see that the percentage of the Gross National Product absorbed by defence does not rise significantly, some increase in cost in absolute terms is to be expected as the national product itself increases.'

In the absence of any significant change in the world situation, therefore, it can be assumed that defence expenditure will remain

[1] This has since been increased by Supplementary Estimates totalling £33 million.

broadly at 7 per cent of the gross national product over the next five years. This is significant because, although changes within the pattern of expenditure are bound to take place, the overall impact of defence expenditure on the economy is unlikely to alter to any great extent, so that the conclusions reached in this survey should retain their validity for a reasonable period of time.

In fact, current defence expenditure as a proportion of the gross national product has not changed greatly in recent years. From a postwar peak of 17·8 per cent of the gross national product in 1946 it fell rapidly until the outbreak of the Korean War, when it rose again to reach a high point of 10·4 per cent in 1952. Since 1952 it has not altered very significantly in absolute terms, but it declined steadily as a proportion of the gross national product until 1961. The changes which have taken place since 1946 are shown in Table 1 on page 3, which also includes all the other items which go to make up total defence expenditure. These figures are taken from the National Income and Expenditure tables and relate to calendar years, but are broadly comparable with the estimates quoted above from the Statements on Defence.

To see in greater detail how the money used for defence is spent it is necessary to return to the Estimates. The Statement on Defence gives an analysis of the expenditure of each of the service and supply departments separately, both in gross and net terms. This is done since expenditure by one department is sometimes paid for by another, so to avoid double counting of these items there is a balancing payment—called an Appropriation-in-Aid—which is deducted from gross expenditure in order to obtain a net figure. In addition, partly for security reasons, certain items of expenditure on production and research are not shown separately and are therefore counted twice, so that a further sum has to be deducted in order to avoid double counting. Thus for 1962–63 gross expenditure is estimated at £2,302·28 million, but this is reduced to the net figure of £1,721·06 million by the deduction of £238·72 million of appropriations-in-aid and a £342·50 million balancing item. The breakdown of this estimated net defence expenditure for 1962–63, together with a comparison with 1961–62, is given in Table 2 on page 4.

The major item of expenditure is production and research, which is estimated at 41 per cent of the total in 1962–63, and this category also showed the greatest increase in absolute terms on 1961–62. Its importance reflects both the high cost and complexity of modern military equipment and the tendency to rely less on men and more on machines. The second largest item is the pay of service personnel followed by the

TABLE 1 *Defence Expenditure in the United Kingdom*

£s million

	1946	1948	1950	1952	1954	1956	1958	1960	1961¹
MILITARY DEFENCE									
Current expenditure on goods and services	1,560	740	820	1,450	1,548	1,621	1,529	1,590	1,735
Gross fixed capital formation at home	n.a.	10	32	100	57	56	57	46	n.a.
Increase in value of stocks	n.a.	n.a.	nil	6	—1	—3	—4	—1	n.a.
Current grants to persons	n.a.	n.a.	nil	nil	1	1	1	2	n.a.
Current grants abroad	n.a.	n.a.	7	15	18	16	14	15	n.a.
Capital grants	n.a.	n.a.	2	2	2	2	2	2	n.a.
Total Military Defence Expenditure	n.a.	n.a.	861	1,573	1,625	1,693	1,599	1,655	n.a.
Total Civil Defence Expenditure²	n.a.	n.a.	2	78	79	4	2	—15	n.a.
Total Expenditure on Defence	n.a.	n.a.	863	1,651	1,704	1,697	1,601	1,640	n.a.
Current Military Expenditure as a percentage of Gross National Product at factor cost (per cent)	17·8	7·1	7·0	10·4	9·7	8·8	7·5	7·1	7·3

¹ Provisional.
² Including any changes in the values of stocks.
n.a. Not available.

Source: National Income and Expenditure Blue Books and Preliminary Estimates 1956 to 1961.

TABLE 2 *Division of the Defence Budget under the Principal Headings*

	1961–1962[1]		1962–1963		Increase+ or Decrease− 1962–1963 on 1961–1962
	Net Expenditure (£ million)	Per cent of Total (per cent)	Net Expenditure (£ million)	Per cent of Total (per cent)	(£ million)
1. Pay, etc. of Service personnel	331·25	20·0	331·95	19·3	+0·70
2. Pay, etc. [of Reserve, Territorial and Auxiliary Forces and grants for administration etc.]	20·10	1·2	20·28	1·2	+0·18
3. Pay, etc. of civilians	245·96	14·9	259·01	15·0	+13·05
4. Movements	55·72	3·4	56·97	3·3	+1·25
5. Supplies:—	(131·61)	(7·9)	(137·18)	(8·0)	(+5·57)
(a) Petrol, oil and lubricants	56·12	3·4	61·32	3·6	+5·20
(b) Food and ration allowance	50·38	3·0	48·33	2·8	−2·05
(c) Fuel and light	20·91	1·3	22·90	1·3	+1·99
(d) Miscellaneous	4·20	0·3	4·63	0·3	+0·43
6. Production and Research[2]	658·85	39·8	705·13	41·0	+46·28
7. Works, buildings and land	111·62	6·7	119·81	7·0	+8·19
8. Miscellaneous effective services	18·64	1·1	23·52	1·4	+4·88
9. Non-effective charges	81·85	4·9	67·21	3·9	−14·64
10. Totals	1,655·60	100·0	1,721·06	100·0	+65·46

Source: Statement on Defence 1961 and 1962.

[1] Excluding the Supplementary Estimates of £33 million.
[2] Includes the cost of development work undertaken by industry under contract, the purchase of stores for research and development establishments and costs of the Royal Ordnance Factories.

pay of civilians. Despite falling numbers the total pay of the Services is rising, and will rise still further as a result of recent and promised pay increases, while the greater reliance on civilians to undertake general duties is a factor making for the increase in the importance of this item in the budget. The growth in expenditure on production and research and the employment of civilians tends to widen, though not necessarily to increase, the impact of defence expenditure on the economy as a whole, and makes its overall effect more difficult to assess. This is important since the greater the difficulty of clearly assessing the impact of defence expenditure, the greater is the likelihood of disarmament leading to unexpected, and possibly adverse, effects on the economy as a whole. The emphasis in this first part of the survey is, therefore, placed on discovering the impact of defence expenditure in these relatively undocumented fields.

THE INTERNATIONAL POSITION

Before going on to the detailed study of defence expenditure in the United Kingdom economy, it is interesting to see how it fits into the world picture of military spending. Such a review is to some extent essential, since it has been assumed for the purposes of this study that disarmament would be general, and although most of the impact of disarmament would be felt within individual countries, there would also be some international effect which should be taken into account. For example, some raw materials, particularly metals, have uses in the armaments field which are not, as yet, matched in civil production. The raw materials in question are mainly exported by under-developed countries which could, to this extent, suffer positive harm if disarmament were to occur. Similarly, the removal of overseas garrisons from under-developed countries would result in a significant loss of revenue to the host countries in a number of instances.

An attempt will be made to consider such points in greater detail in the second part of this survey, and, at this stage, the international analysis will be confined to considering the United Kingdom's defence expenditure in a world setting.

The United Nations Survey on the Economic and Social Consequences of Disarmament, quoted earlier, put current world expenditure on military account at about £43,000 million a year, and it seems clear that it is rising rather than falling at present. To indicate just what a sum of this magnitude means—it is roughly twice the gross national product of the United Kingdom—the report made the following comparisons.

'This figure (£43,000 million) is equivalent to about 8–9 per cent of the world's annual output of all goods and services; it is at least two-thirds of—and according to some estimates may be of the same order of magnitude as—the entire national income of all the under-developed countries. It is close to the value of the world's annual exports of all commodities and it corresponds to about one-half of the total resources set aside each year for gross capital formation throughout the world'.

The report went on to estimate the world's armed forces at about 20 million persons, and the total of all persons directly and indirectly employed as a result of military expenditure at possibly over 50 million.

Of greater importance, however, was the assessment that about 85 per cent of the world's military expenditure is accounted for by seven countries—Canada, West Germany, France, the United Kingdom and the United States in the West and China and Russia in the East. The total military expenditure of the under-developed countries as a whole, on the other hand, was put at one-tenth of that of 'the industrial private enterprise economies'. In terms of productive resources, therefore, and to a lesser extent manpower, the majority of resources released by disarmament would be concentrated in only a few countries.

The following table indicates the extent to which the countries in the North Atlantic Treaty Organisation—the countries with which the most significant comparisons with the United Kingdom are possible—devote their national resources to defence. When looking at this table it should be borne in mind that the almost general decline in the percentages since 1955 does not necessarily indicate a fall in the actual levels of defence expenditure.

The proportion of gross national product devoted to defence in each country is, however, only a rough guide to its comparative importance. This is partly because of price differences and partly because the make-up of the defence budget differs quite widely from country to country. Nevertheless, the countries have been ranked according to the proportion of the gross national product devoted to defence expenditure in 1960. It shows the United States with the highest proportion, followed by the United Kingdom and France. Next come West Germany, Greece and Canada, and it is interesting to note that with the exception of Greece these were the five western countries included in the seven top-spenders in the United Nations' report.

TABLE 3 *The Percentage of Gross National Product at factor cost accounted for by Defence Expenditure*

1950	1955	1960	North Atlantic Treaty Organisation Countries
5·5	11·0	9·2	United States
7·0	8·9	7·1	United Kingdom
6·7	5·8	6·9	France
5·2[1]	4·0[1]	6·8	West Germany
7·0	6·4	6·2	Greece
3·6	7·8	5·3	Canada
4·7	6·2	4·3	Netherlands
6·4	6·1	4·3	Turkey
3·3	4·6	4·1	Portugal
2·4	4·0	3·5	Norway
4·6	4·6	3·4	Italy
2·3	3·8	3·2	Belgium
1·7	3·5	2·9	Denmark
n.a.	2·7	1·8	Luxembourg

[1] Occupation costs only up to mid-1955.
Source: O.E.E.C. General Statistics.

Chapter 2

Defence and Employment

THE NUMBERS EMPLOYED ON DEFENCE WORK

As a first step towards estimating in detail the way in which defence expenditure affects the economy, it is helpful to discover the number of persons directly employed on defence work. To do this three broad groups of people must be added together—the numbers in the armed services, the personnel of the service and supply departments and the numbers of people engaged on defence production and research work. Of these three only the first can be given with certainty, and even in this instance the figures may slightly overestimate the importance of this employment to the United Kingdom. This is because a number of Commonwealth and Irish nationals come to Britain to join the forces, and they might return to their own countries in the event of disarmament. For practical purposes, however, this reservation can be ignored.

Employment in the service and supply departments is also known, but in this case there would be substantial double counting if the figures were taken at their face value. This is because government employees engaged on production and research work for the armed forces are also included in the industrial analysis which is prepared by the Ministry of Labour. The numbers concerned can only be estimated roughly from the Estimates for each department, but an additional check was obtained from figures supplied by the departments, breaking down the government workers engaged on defence production and research by type and by the area of the country in which they carried out their work. As a result of this information the published figures of employees in the service and supply departments were reduced by 150,000. In addition, as the Ministry of Aviation carries out both civil and military duties, it was necessary to deduct a further 10,000 from the figure obtained above in order to take account of this fact. This gives a total corrected figure for the service and supply departments of 200,000 at end-May, 1961.

TABLE 4 *The Industry Pattern of Employment on Defence Contracts in Manufacturing Industry at End May 1961*

	Great Britain			Northern Ireland	United Kingdom		
	Employment on Defence Contracts						
	Numbers Employed[1] (thousands)	Percentage of Total Employment	Total Employment[1] (thousands)	Estimated Employment on Defence Contracts[2] (thousands)	Estimated Employment on Defence Contracts[2] (thousands)	Total Employment[1] (thousands)	
Explosives and Fireworks	10·8	33·0	32·7	nil	10·8	32·7	
Iron and Steel (General)	13·0	4·2	307·3	nil	13·0	307·3	
Steel Tubes	2·4	4·3	56·1	nil	2·4	56·2	
Light Metals	4·1	7·1	57·7	nil	4·1	57·7	
Metal-Working Machine Tools	3·3	3·5	93·3	nil	3·3	93·6	
Engineers' Small Tools and Gauges	2·1	3·8	54·7	nil	2·1	54·8	
Industrial Engines	3·0	6·8	44·1	nil	3·0	44·2	
Other Machinery	5·3	1·5	345·7	nil	5·3	348·4	
Ordnance and Small Arms	23·3	73·7	31·6	0·1	23·4	31·8	
Other Mechanical Engineering not elsewhere specified	8·7	4·2	208·3	0·1	8·8	209·9	
Scientific, Surgical and Photographic Instruments etc.	10·4	7·7	134·8	0·1	10·5	136·0	
Electrical Machinery	7·5	3·4	223·8	0·2	7·7	226·1	
Insulated Wires and Cables	2·4	3·8	63·4	nil	2·4	63·7	
Telegraph and Telephone Apparatus	4·7	7·1	66·0	nil	4·7	66·1	
Radio and Other Electronic Apparatus	39·5	16·7	237·2	0·7	40·2	240·9	
Other Electrical Goods	7·4	5·0	147·3	nil	7·4	147·5	
Shipbuilding and Ship Repairing	11·3	6·1	184·4	0·9	12·2	200·0	
Marine Engineering	8·6	12·6	68·3	0·9	9·5	75·5	
Motor Vehicle Manufacturing	8·0	1·9	414·4	nil	8·0	415·1	
Aircraft Manufacturing and Repairing	136·9	45·9	298·1	2·9	139·8	304·6	
Metal Industries not elsewhere specified	8·1	2·2	367·5	nil	8·1	368·4	
Rubber	2·3	1·8	125·0	nil	2·3	125·4	
Total—above Industries	323·1	9·1	3,561·5	5·9	329·0	3,605·9	
Total—all other Manufacturing Industries	33·1	0·6	5,305·5	0·9	34·0	5,450·7	
Total Manufacturing Industries	356·2	4·0	8,867·1	6·8	363·0	9,056·6	

[1] Source: Ministry of Labour. [2] E.I.U. Estimates.

For details of the numbers employed on defence production and research the main source of information is the twice yearly surveys carried out by the Ministry of Labour. These cover manufacturing industry in Great Britain and, as stated above, include government employees. To this figure must be added the persons employed on defence contracts by the Admiralty and atomic energy establishments, which are excluded from the manufacturing industry breakdown, which gives a figure of 408,700 at end-May, 1961.

The figure obtained, however, refers only to manufacturing industry in Great Britain, so that further adjustments have to be made. To obtain an estimate of comparable employment in the United Kingdom as a whole it has been assumed that for each industry shown separately the same proportion of employees are engaged on defence work as in Great Britain, and from the resulting figures 'employment by industry on defence contracts in Northern Ireland was also calculated. The figures obtained are set out in detail in Table 4 on page 9.

Finally, it is necessary to add an estimate of the persons employed in non-manufacturing industry who are directly engaged on defence work. These are most likely to be employed in two industries—building and transport. Net expenditure on works, buildings and lands in the Combined Defence Estimates for 1961–62 was nearly £112 million, compared with a total value of constructional work in Great Britain during 1961 of £2,851 million. Part of the defence total of £112 million will, of course, not relate to building activity, and even if this could be eliminated a proportion of the building work proper (which includes maintenance) is almost certainly carried out by service personnel. Nevertheless, there is a substantial amount of new building work—particularly on married quarters—being carried out at present for the Services, and if 1 per cent of the construction labour force of 1,590,000 persons in May 1961 is taken as being engaged on defence work this is probably not too unrealistic. It is even more difficult to make a reasonable estimate of direct employment on defence works in the fields of transport and communications, so it has been arbitrarily assumed that in these industries, and all the other non-manufacturing industries combined, it does not exceed 10,000. This gives a total of direct employment on defence work in non-manufacturing industry of some 25,000 persons.

The net result of all these calculations and assumptions is set out in the following table.

TABLE 5 *Direct Employment on Defence, End-May, 1961*

thousands

478	H.M. Forces
200	Service and Supply Departments (net)
440	Production and Research
1,118	Total Direct Employment

The total of direct employment on defence of 1,118,000 persons at end-May, 1961 was 4·5 per cent of the total working population[1] at that time, compared with the 7·3 per cent of the gross national product in 1961 as a whole which went on defence expenditure. If defence accounted for the same proportion of the total working population as of the gross national product then some 1,800,000 persons would have been employed on defence during 1961. It is, in fact, unlikely that the proportion of defence expenditure to gross national product would be exactly matched by the employment figures; differences in the import content of defence expenditure and the gross national product alone are likely to result in different patterns of employment. Nevertheless, the additional workers suggested by the gross national product calculation do give an indication of the level of secondary employment which results from defence expenditure.

This comes about, for example, from the use of fuel and light by the Services, the service and supply departments and the industries engaged on defence production and research, the transport of raw materials to factories and the distribution of the finished products and all the other ancillary services used by those directly employed on defence work. The numbers employed in any one region, or by any one defence industry, are unlikely to be very large, and they will be spread out over a number of different industries and trades. Nevertheless, in the event of unemployment resulting from the sudden running down of defence contracts, there would clearly be repercussions on the level of employment in these secondary industries. At best, the lower level of activity could lead to a reduction in business confidence which would aggravate the difficulties facing the defence industries, and in certain instances (for example in garrison towns) it might lead to further serious

[1] The total working population represents the estimated number of persons aged 15 and over who work for pay or gain, or register themselves as available for such work. In addition to the Services and all those in employment, therefore, it also includes the temporarily stopped and the wholly unemployed.

unemployment. Despite the difficulties involved in quantifying the level of secondary employment on defence it is, therefore, clearly a factor which should be taken into consideration, and attention is paid to it wherever possible in the individual industry studies which follow.

THE INDUSTRIAL AND REGIONAL PATTERN OF DEFENCE EMPLOYMENT

The overall level of employment on defence, though important, is of much less significance than the distribution of this employment throughout the economy. Clearly, if defence employment is spread out over the country in the same proportion as the population as a whole, and the industrial workers are distributed by industry in accordance with the total employment figures, then the impact of disarmament would almost certainly be less than if defence work were concentrated in one or two areas and in one or two industries.

One factor of importance is the siting of Service establishments in the United Kingdom, and this is largely a matter of historical accident. Moreover, their importance to the economic life of the areas in which they are situated varies enormously, making generalisations impossible, although there is no doubt of their significance in certain cases. To obtain an indication of the extent of local dependence on Service garrisons and the problems which might be met on their removal, interviews and research were carried out in two towns, Aldershot and Chatham. A fuller account of the results obtained is given in Appendix A, but it is briefly summarised here.

As perhaps would be expected, the pattern was very different in the two towns. Aldershot, a prosperous and growing community, for the most part viewed the prospect of disarmament causing the run down of its garrison with equanimity, although it was realised that certain sectional interests would suffer—for example the cinemas and public houses. In Chatham, on the other hand, where the level of unemployment is above the national average, the position was almost the reverse. In fact, Chatham is not a garrison town to any significant extent; defence employment now mainly centres on the naval dockyard. The town has already suffered as a result of the closing of naval establishments and of the nearby dockyard at Sheerness, and could well become a depressed area in need of special assistance in the event of the dockyard being closed. It seems clear, therefore, that every such area should be considered separately, with particular reference to the impact of the remainder of defence work in the region. This was not possible within the scope of the present survey.

Of the 200,000 civil servants engaged directly on defence work (excluding those engaged on production and research), the largest single group, probably just under one-half, is concentrated in the London area. It comprises the senior administrative officers together with their staffs of specialist, executive and clerical workers. Many such workers are in short supply in the London area, particularly in the lower grades, and they would probably have little difficulty in finding alternative employment. In any event, the services of all the persons concerned would be required for a significant period of time in order to administer the running down of the defence programme, and this would provide an opportunity to absorb staff gradually into other government work, as well as reducing the numbers involved by normal wastage. Probably the greatest problems would be faced by the older, relatively senior workers, in the same way as it has been found more difficult to place the older and more senior officers of the armed services in comparable civil posts when they have been compulsorily retired. Some special assistance, on similar lines to that used for Service officers, should prevent undue hardship in cases where it is not possible to absorb personnel into the civil departments.

The remainder of these civil servants are employed at Service establishments, training camps, military headquarters and specialist centres throughout the United Kingdom. They are made up, in broadly equal proportions, of administrative, technical, executive and clerical staff on the one hand, and industrial workers, the majority of whom are locally engaged, on the other. Their prospects of obtaining other employment will vary from region to region, as was seen above in the comments on the situation in Aldershot and Chatham, and it is not possible to make a general assessment of the situation. However, it would seem that the industrial workers, many of whom are unskilled, will have the greatest difficulty in finding alternative employment.

Finally, it is necessary to consider the area pattern of industrial employment on defence production and research work. A detailed breakdown of employment by industry in each of the standard industrial regions was supplied by the Ministry of Labour, showing the position at end-May, 1961. These figures, which refer only to manufacturing industry, include employment on defence production and research work both by private industry and in Royal Ordnance Factories and other government establishments. They exclude Admiralty employees and defence workers at the atomic energy establishments. The figures are given in detail in Table 6 on page 14.

TABLE 6 *Numbers Employed on Defence Contracts—Period End May, 1961* (Thousands)

Lon-don and South East	East and South	South West	Mid-land	North Mid-land	East and West Rid-ings	North West	North	Scot-land	Wales	Great Brit-ain	INDUSTRY
0·1	nil	nil	0·4	0·1	nil	5·0	nil	2·1	3·1	10·8	Explosives and Fireworks
nil	nil	nil	1·2	1·3	3·7	0·8	2·3	1·1	2·6	13·0	Iron and Steel (general)
0·1	0·1	nil	1·2	0·4	nil	nil	nil	0·5	0·1	2·4	Steel tubes
0·1	0·9	nil	2·5	0·1	0·1	0·1	0·2	0·1	nil	4·1	Light metals
0·3	1·0	0·2	0·8	0·1	0·3	0·3	nil	0·3	nil	3·3	Metal-working Machine Tools
0·4	0·4	0·5	0·5	nil	0·3	0·5	nil	nil	nil	2·1	Engineers' Small Tools and Gauges
0·1	nil	2·4	0·5	nil	nil	nil	0·8	nil	0·5	3·0	Industrial Engines
1·4	0·7	0·2	1·1	0·5	0·1	1·0	0·2	0·6	0·2	5·3	Other Machinery
6·3	1·4	nil	3·7	1·7	1·2	4·5	3·7	nil	0·8	23·3	Ordnance and Small Arms
2·1	1·6	1·3	0·6	nil	1·0	nil	0·1	nil	0·3	8·7	Other Mechanical Engineering not elsewhere specified
6·4	0·9	0·7	0·1	0·2	0·5	0·1	0·1	1·5	nil	10·4	Scientific, Surgical and Photographic Instruments etc.
1·3	2·1	0·1	1·7	nil	1·3	0·2	0·3	0·5	0·5	7·5	Electrical Machinery
0·4	0·2	nil	nil	nil	nil	0·5	0·8	nil	0·5	2·4	Insulated Wires and Cables
0·6	0·5	nil	2·0	0·4	nil	1·0	0·2	nil	nil	4·7	Telegraph and Telephone Apparatus
15·7	6·6	1·8	1·6	2·3	0·1	4·8	1·8	4·6	0·2	39·5	Radio and Other Electronic Apparatus
0·4	0·4	0·3	0·4	0·1	nil	0·6	0·6	0·1	0·1	7·4	Other Electrical Goods
0·2	1·6	0·1	nil	0·1	nil	0·8	nil	3·7	nil	11·3	Shipbuilding and Ship-repairing
nil	2·0	nil	nil	nil	nil	3·7	0·4	2·0	0·5	8·6	Marine Engineering
0·5	0·9	0·6	4·4	0·1	0·2	nil	nil	nil	nil	8·0	Motor Vehicle Manufacturing
17·0	21·6	26·5	18·3	9·8	5·1	1·3	0·2	7·0	0·4	136·9	Aircraft Manufacturing and Repairing
2·4	0·2	nil	2·9	0·3	0·4	0·6	nil	0·8	0·5	8·1	Metal Industries not elsewhere specified
0·5	0·5	0·2	0·8	nil	nil	0·1	nil	0·1	0·1	2·3	Rubber
60·1	44·1	34·7	45·4	18·0	13·3	61·0	12·1	24·5	9·9	323·1	Total—above Industries
5·0	3·8	2·9	4·3	1·8	2·6	8·1	1·1	2·7	0·8	33·1	Total—all other Manufacturing Industries
65·1	47·9	37·6	49·7	19·8	15·9	69·1	13·2	27·2	10·7	356·2	Total—Manufacturing Industries

Source: Ministry of Labour

The industries most affected are aircraft (38·4 per cent of total employment on defence work in manufacturing industry in Great Britain), radio and other electronic apparatus (11·1 per cent), ordnance and small arms together with explosives and fireworks (9·6 per cent) and shipbuilding and ship-repairing together with marine engineering (5·6 per cent). The shipbuilding figure is, of course, affected by the exclusion of the Admiralty workers, which means that its importance as a defence industry is understated by these figures.

The area pattern of employment by industry is considered in greater detail in the later sections dealing with particular industries. It is, however, interesting to compare the area pattern of defence employment in manufacturing industry as a whole with the total pattern of employment in Great Britain, and this is done in Table 7 on page 16. In the previous section, dealing with the total direct impact of defence expenditure on employment, estimates were also made of the level of direct employment in Northern Ireland and the United Kingdom as a whole (see Table 4) and these have also been included in the area analysis in Table 7.

It can be seen from Table 7 that the extent of defence employment in manufacturing industry ranges from 9·6 per cent of total employment in the south-western region down to 1·8 per cent in the East and West Ridings. The average for manufacturing industry as a whole is 4·0 per cent. In terms of the numbers involved, however, the two most important regions are clearly the north-western and London and the south-east, with 19·4 per cent and 18·3 per cent respectively of the total in Great Britain. Only in the north-west does this proportion exceed the region's share of total employment in manufacturing industry—and the north-west also has a slightly above average level of unemployment. This region might be expected to suffer more than most, therefore, in the event of disarmament. Other regions where the proportion of defence employment exceeds the region's share of total employment are the eastern and southern, south western and (marginally) the Midlands. None of these are regions of above average unemployment. In the two areas of high unemployment, Scotland and Northern Ireland,[1] defence employment accounts for only 3·6 per cent

---

[1] The analysis of the questionnaires sent out by the Unit (see Chapter 3) indicates that the estimate of numbers employed on defence work in Northern Ireland, as calculated in Table 4, is an understatement. It is not possible to quote the actual figures, but a more realistic estimate of the proportion in manufacturing industry employed on defence work in Northern Ireland would probably be 5 per cent. However, an upward revision of this order only marginally affects the conclusions reached above.

TABLE 7 *The Area Pattern of Employment on Defence Contracts in Manufacturing Industry at End-May 1961*

	Numbers employed on Defence Contracts	Percentage of Total Employed persons	Total Employment in each Region	The Percentage of Total Employment in each Region		Unemployment in each Region[1]	
				On Defence contracts	All Employed persons	Numbers	As a Percentage of Total Employment
	thousands	per cent	thousands	per cent	per cent	thousands	per cent
London and South East	65·1	3·5	1,886·4	18·3	21·3	48·0	0·8
Eastern and Southern	47·9	5·5	866·3	13·4	9·8	22·3	0·9
South-Western	37·6	9·6	392·4	10·6	4·4	15·4	1·2
Midland	49·7	4·0	1,232·1	14·0	13·9	20·8	0·9
North-Midland	19·8	2·9	682·2	5·6	7·7	15·8	1·0
East and West Ridings	15·9	1·8	365·4	4·5	9·8	16·3	0·9
North-Western	69·1	4·9	1,419·4	19·4	16·0	44·5	1·5
Northern	13·2	2·9	456·6	3·7	5·1	29·7	2·3
Scotland	27·2	3·6	760·3	7·6	8·6	64·9	3·0
Wales	10·7	3·5	305·9	3·0	3·4	21·6	2·2
Total—Great Britain	356·2	4·0	8,867·1	100·0	100·0	299·3	1·3
Great Britain	356·2	4·0	8,867·1	98·1	97·9	299·3	1·3
Northern Ireland	6·8	3·6	189·5	1·9	2·1	35·5	7·3
United Kingdom	363·0	4·0	9,056·6	100·0	100·0	334·8	1·5

[1] All industry—mid-May figures.
Source: Ministry of Labour and E.I.U. Estimates.

of the total employment in manufacturing industry, and in both cases the regions account for a lower proportion of defence employment than of total employment.

It seems clear from this analysis that no region is liable to be hit unduly hard by the ending of defence contracts, though it is likely to be a greater problem in areas where unemployment is highest. It is encouraging, therefore, that employment on defence work is below average in these regions, and in the region most likely to be affected, the north-western, unemployment is only slightly higher than the national average. Though individual towns and companies may be vulnerable to changes in defence spending, and special assistance in particular to certain towns might be necessary, it seems reasonable to assume that no specifically regional problems are likely to emerge in the event of disarmament.

Chapter 3

Defence Expenditure and the Firm

In addition to the estimates of direct employment and the regional impact of defence expenditure given above, which are based on official sources of information, it was felt that to obtain a complete picture it is essential to have some indication as to how individual firms are affected by defence expenditure. For, in the same way as the effects of any change in defence expenditure would be greater or smaller depending upon whether its impact was concentrated or widespread by industry and area, so it would also tend to be greater if a small number of firms were fully committed to defence work than if defence contracts formed only a relatively minor proportion of the output of a wide range of companies.

To obtain details of the impact of defence expenditure on individual companies a brief questionnaire was sent out to a selection of companies in the industries known to carry out the major part of defence work. The industries approached were aircraft, armaments, clothing, chemicals, electrical engineering, electronics, general engineering, instruments, oil and petroleum, shipbuilding and marine engineering and vehicles. This was in no sense a random sample, since it was felt that within the limits of time and cost to which we were working, it would not have been possible to obtain sufficient positive replies using random sampling methods. Efforts were made, therefore, to try and ensure that the companies asked for information were, in fact, likely to undertake defence work, although, except in cases where it is common knowledge that companies are so engaged, no official information is available on this subject. Firms of all sizes likely to fall in this category were selected, in order that as wide a range of businesses as possible should be represented.

The majority of the questionnaires were sent out on September 20, 1961 and the remainder at irregular intervals after that date—mainly as a result of requests or suggestions received from companies originally approached. A copy of the questionnaire and the accompanying letter are given in Appendix B. All concerns which were sent the questionnaire also received a letter from the Ministry of Defence stating that The Economist Intelligence Unit Limited had been authorised to undertake the research and setting out the conditions under which the Unit was working, and this letter was undoubtedly in part responsible for the high level of response.

In total, 434 questionnaires were sent out. Some companies, however, completed separate questionnaires for their subsidiaries which undertook different types of work and could not readily be consolidated into a company total. For this reason, the total of companies investigated amounted to 455. An analysis of the replies received is given in the following table.

TABLE 8 *The Response to the Questionnaire sent to Individual Companies*

Number	Per cent of total	
251	55·2	Replies received of which:
142	31·2	Carried out defence work
87	19·1	Did not carry out defence work
22	4·8	Refused or gave no definite answer
204	44·8	Did not reply
455	100·0	Total questionnaires

The detailed analysis which follows is confined to the 142 companies carrying out defence contracts at the time when they completed the questionnaires. It is necessary to stress this point of time, since a number of companies stated that, because of the irregular nature of defence work, their replies did not reflect their average dependence on defence contracts in recent years. However, most of the companies concerned were reluctant or unable to assess this average level, so it was decided not to try to take account of any fluctuations, but to relate the results to one period of time. The completed questionnaires were in fact received at intervals during the period end-September, 1961 to March, 1962, although the majority related to the position during the final quarter of 1961.

Another factor which could affect the results is that a number of companies were unaware of the final end-use of their products. This is not important in the case of companies which stated that they carried out defence work, as for the most part they either knew, or were able to estimate with accuracy, the amount of their turnover represented by defence contracts. To this extent the results as analysed in the following tables can be taken as an accurate guide to the impact of defence expenditure on the companies concerned.

A number of companies, however, which replied that they did not carry out defence contracts, qualified their answers by pointing out that they were unaware of the final end-use of their products. The companies concerned were mainly suppliers of raw materials, such as metals and chemicals, and manufacturers of components acting on a sub-contract, or sub-sub-contract basis. In the case of suppliers of raw materials it is unlikely where special grades or types of products are involved that the companies concerned would be unaware of their eventual end-use. The usage of ordinary grades of materials by the defence industries results in the secondary employment commented upon in the section on employment above, and it is impossible to estimate the impact this has on individual companies. In the absence of any definite evidence to the contrary, however, it seems reasonable to assume that it is not of major significance to particular firms.

The position seems less clear in the case of the manufacture of aircraft and electronic components. Sub-contract work can amount to two-thirds of the value of a particular contract in the aircraft field, though the aircraft company concerned will probably not dispose of all this work itself. It appears from the replies received that in a number of instances the components concerned are used in both civil and military aircraft, with possibly other uses as well, and that no special security regulations are involved in their manufacture. As component firms are often small, employing less than 100 workers, and tend to rely on a relatively narrow range of products, it seems possible that a number of such firms may be dependent on defence expenditure for a significant proportion of their annual sales without being aware of the fact. Apart from drawing attention to this, however, there is little else that can be done, as it has not proved possible to obtain definite information as to the numbers of firms or workers involved.

The proportion of turnover accounted for by defence contracts was 10 per cent or below for 80 of the 142 companies engaged on defence work, or 56·3 per cent of the total companies analysed (Table 9). Moreover, the category 'up to 10 per cent of turnover' included the largest single number of companies in each of the separate size ranges, with the one exception of the group with 3,001–4,000 employees. At

TABLE 9 *The Proportion of Company Turnover Represented by Defence Contracts*

Number of Companies in each Category

Proportion of Turnover Represented by Defence Contracts						
Up to 10 per cent	11–25 per cent	26–50 per cent	51–75 per cent	76–100 per cent	Total number of companies	Size of companies
						Companies employing:-
6	1	1	nil	nil	8	Up to 100 persons
6	1	3	1	1	12	101–200
8	nil	1	2	nil	11	201–300
3	1	3	nil	nil	7	301–400
4	3	2	2	1	12	401–500
5	3	1	nil	nil	9	501–750
5	2	nil	2	nil	9	751–1,000
14	1	1	2	1	19	1,001–2,000
6	2	nil	1	2	11	2,001–3,000
1	2	2	nil	2	7	3,001–4,000
2	1	nil	nil	nil	3	4,001–5,000
12	nil	1	1	2	16	5,001–10,000
8	3	5	1	1	18	More than 10,000 persons
80	20	20	12	10	142	Total all Companies
56·3	14·1	14·1	8·5	7·0	100	Percentage Breakdown

the other end of the scale, where defence contracts accounted for more than 75 per cent of turnover, there were only ten firms, or 7·0 per cent of the total investigated, and eight of these employed more than 1,000 workers. It is also the case that the majority of companies whose defence contracts accounted for over 50 per cent of turnover were fairly large concerns, 59 per cent employing more than 1,000 workers. In total, however, companies carrying out defence work were fairly evenly distributed by size, and 48 per cent, or 68 firms, employed 1,000 or less workers.

Six companies did not give details of employment; the remaining 136 employed between them 749,928 persons of whom 174,964, or 23·3 per cent, were wholly (or mostly) engaged on defence work. The numbers engaged wholly (or mostly) on defence work thus account for nearly 50 per cent of total manufacturing employment on defence (see page 9); this high proportion indicates that the overall results of the questionnaire are likely to be reliable. Full details, with a breakdown by size of company, are given in Table 10. Once again no clear pattern by size of firm emerged, though in overall terms the predominance of the largest concerns employing over 10,000 workers was readily apparent. In total, the 18 companies concerned accounted for 131,585 of the 174,964 workers engaged wholly (or mostly) on defence work, or 75·2 per cent, which was slightly higher than the proportion of the total employment accounted for by the 18 companies concerned.

This is reasonably encouraging from the point of view of the problems likely to emerge in the event of disarmament, since only in two instances did defence contracts account for more than 50 per cent of the turnover of these 18 firms; one was in the 51 to 75 per cent range and the other derived over 76 per cent of its turnover from defence work. In addition, it was found that, for the most part, the larger firms were more diversified than the average, and, therefore, had ready-made outlets on which to concentrate their resources in the event of defence contracts ending. Nevertheless, because of their sheer size, the problems likely to be involved are considerable, since it is these companies which employ the majority of the highly specialised labour, equipment and plant used for defence purposes, which is not readily transferable to other types of work. Moreover, defence contracts often form the staple business of the firms concerned, and are the source from which their other activities stem, so that their room for manoeuvre is less than might at first seem to be the case. These problems are considered in greater detail in the individual industry sections which follow later in this study.

TABLE 10 *The Proportion of Total Employees Engaged on Defence Work*

Persons engaged wholly (or mostly) on Defence Work		Total employment	Companies included	Size of companies
number	per cent	number	number	
				Companies employing:–
30	7·7	389	8	Up to 100 persons
437	27·1	1,613	11	101–200
466	15·8	2,954	11	201–300
333	15·7	2,124	6	301–400
1,122	20·1	5,590	12	401–500
269	4·6	5,830	9	501–750
1,443	19·0	7,595	9	751–1,000
4,555	16·8	27,153	18	1,001–2,000
5,847	22·5	26,034	11	2,001–3,000
7,213	29·7	24,298	7	3,001–4,000
650	7·6	8,600	2	4,001–5,000
21,014	20·3	103,266	14	5,001–10,000
131,585	24·6	534,482	18	More than 10,000 persons
174,964	23·3	749,928	136	Total all Companies

Finally, an analysis has been made of the regions in which the companies carry out their defence work. The numbers involved are higher than the total of companies replying, since many of the larger concerns operate in more than one region of the country, and the details are set out in Table 11. It shows that the most important region is the London and south-eastern, with nearly twice as many firms as in any of the others, followed by the eastern and southern (combined), the midland and the north-western regions. These four regions are also the main areas of employment on defence work as shown in Table 6, (which related to Great Britain) though in a different order of importance—the north-western first, followed by the London and south-eastern, the midland and the eastern and southern in that order. The reason for the main discrepancy—the dominance of the London and south-eastern region in the company analysis—is due to the large number of relatively small firms which are situated in this area. These are mainly manufacturers of aircraft and electronics components,

TABLE 11 Regions of the United Kingdom in which Defence Contracts are carried out

Firms employing

Region	Up to 200 Persons number	Percent of Total	201–500 number	Percent of Total	501–1,000 number	Percent of Total	1,001–5,000 number	Percent of Total	5,001–10,000 number	Percent of Total	Over 10,000 number	Percent of Total	Total number	Percent of Total
Northern	nil	nil	nil	nil	1	4·8	4	7·7	2	5·7	4	7·1	11	5·0
East & West Ridings	nil	nil	1	2·9	3	14·3	2	3·8	1	2·9	4	7·1	11	5·0
North-Midland	1	4·5	2	5·7	nil	nil	nil	nil	3	8·6	4	7·1	10	4·5
Eastern	nil	nil	3	8·6	nil	nil	7	13·5	1	2·9	4	7·1	15	6·8
London & South Eastern	14	63·6	13	37·1	4	19·0	13	25·0	8	22·9	9	16·1	61	27·6
Southern	3	13·6	3	8·6	1	4·8	2	3·8	3	8·6	5	8·9	17	7·7
South-Western	1	4·5	3	8·6	2	9·5	3	5·8	2	5·7	3	5·4	14	6·3
Wales	nil	nil	nil	nil	1	4·8	2	3·8	1	2·9	3	5·4	7	3·2
Midland	2	9·1	6	17·1	4	19·0	3	5·8	9	25·7	7	12·5	31	14·0
North-Western	1	4·5	2	5·7	3	14·3	8	15·4	2	5·7	6	10·7	22	10·0
Scotland	nil	nil	1	2·9	2	9·5	8	15·4	1	2·9	5	8·9	17	7·7
Northern Ireland	nil	nil	1	2·9	nil	nil	nil	nil	2	5·7	2	3·6	5	2·3
Total United Kingdom	22	100	35	100	21	100	52	100	35	100	56	100	221	100

and of the total establishments employing up to 200 persons, 63·6 per cent were in London and the south-east. If allowance is made for this fact, the fair degree of correlation between the regional analysis by company and that by total employment provides confirmation of the validity of the results of the questionnaire.

The other questions on which information was requested were the finance of research expenditure, the transferability of resources and the problems likely to be incurred in the event of disarmament. The answers to the first of these questions are considered in the following chapter dealing with defence expenditure and research. The replies to the questions about the transferability of resources and the problems likely to emerge if defence contracts were ended, were, in part at least, specific to the industries concerned. They have, therefore, been considered under the separate industry analyses which follow, and are not repeated here.

Chapter 4

Defence and Research

The latest available estimates of expenditure on research in the United Kingdom relate to the financial year 1958–59, and were given in the annual report of the Advisory Council on Scientific Policy 1959–60, (Cmnd. 1167). (To avoid unnecessary repetition, throughout this section the term research covers both 'research and development' unless otherwise qualified.) Total expenditure on research in that year is estimated at £477·8 million, compared with £300 million in 1955–56, an increase of nearly 60 per cent. As a proportion of the gross national product research expenditure rose from 1·7 per cent in 1955–56 to 2·3 per cent in 1958–59.

Table 12 on page 27, which is taken from the annual reports for 1956–57 and 1959–60, shows research expenditure broken down in two different ways—by the sources of funds used and by the organisations which carried out the research. It can be seen from this table that defence expenditure provided £234·3 million of the funds for research in 1958–59, or 49·0 per cent of the total. This was £56·8 million higher than in 1955–56, but despite this increase defence expenditure declined in importance as a source of funds over the three years by some ten percentage points. For while defence expenditure on research rose by 32·0 per cent between 1955–56 and 1958–59, non-defence expenditure rose by 98·8 per cent. Another significant change over the three years was that total government expenditure as a source of funds declined from 74·7 per cent of the total in 1955–56 to 66·9 per cent in 1958–59, while private industry's contribution rose from 22·8 per cent to 28·5 per cent of the total.

Private industry is mainly responsible for the carrying out of research in the United Kingdom, although in contrast to the changes that have taken place in the sources of funds, private industry declined in impor-

TABLE 12 *Expenditure on Research and Development in the United Kingdom*

	Sources of Funds				Cost of Research and Development carried out			
	1955–1956		1958–1959		1955–1956		1958–1959	
	£million	per cent	£million	per cent	£million	per cent	£million	per cent
1. Government¹								
(a) Defence	177·5	59·2	234·3	49·0	65·7	21·9	102·9	21·6
(b) Civil	34·5	11·5	67·9	14·2	12·3	4·1	42·9	9·0
(c) Research councils	12·0	4·0	17·6	3·7	10·0	3·3	13·1	2·7
Total	224·0	74·7	319·8	66·9	88·0	29·3	158·9	33·3
2. Public corporations	4·0	1·3	7·8	1·6	4·0	1·3	6·9	1·4
3. Private industry	68·3	22·8	136·0	28·5	185·0	61·7	266·3²	55·8
4. Research associations	nil	nil	nil	nil	4·9	1·6	6·4	1·3
5. Universities	0·5	0·2	1·5	0·3	14·4	4·8	23·3	4·8
6. Other organisations	3·2	1·1	12·7	2·7	3·7	1·2	16·0	3·4
Total	300·0	100·0	477·8	100·0	300·0	100·0	477·8	100·0

¹ Includes the Atomic Energy Authority.
² Made up of £265·0 million for manufacturing industry and £1·3 million for the building and contracting industries. It differs from the figures compiled by the Department of Scientific and Industrial Research in that it excludes depreciation and payment to outside bodies.
Source: Annual reports of the Advisory Council on Scientific Policy, 1956–1957 and 1959–1960.

tance as an undertaker of research, accounting for 55·8 per cent of the total in 1958–59 as against 61·7 per cent in 1955–56. The proportion of the £266·3 million of research carried out by industry which is paid for by defence cannot be assessed with complete accuracy. However, total government outpayments to industry for research in 1958–59 are known to have been £154 million and, as the value of civil research contracts let out to industry is relatively small, industry probably received at least £130 million for research from defence expenditure.

The Department of Scientific and Industrial Research (D.S.I.R.), which estimated research expenditure by manufacturing industry in 1958 at £296·7 million, also stated that less than half this total was provided for out of defence contracts. (For the difference between the D.S.I.R. figures and those of the Advisory Council on Scientific Policy see the note to Table 12, page 27.) The D.S.I.R. figures provide an industry breakdown of research expenditure, with estimates of the numbers of qualified workers involved. A summary of their results is given in Table 13, page 29. As perhaps would be expected, the main concentration of research is in the science based industries—particularly chemicals, electrical engineering and aircraft—and the D.S.I.R. estimates that 80 per cent of defence contracts for research were let to the latter two industries. They also point out, however, that the methods of accounting for defence contracts tend to cost to development expenditure items which in other fields might be costed to production, so that the comparative importance of defence research is probably overstated.

Although these figures are now out-of-date (a new enquiry is currently under way) it would appear that defence expenditure on research has not changed greatly in kind since 1958, though it has risen slightly. A more recent publication, 'The Management and Control of Research and Development', H.M.S.O. 1961, stated in a chapter dealing with defence research that about £240 million[1] was allocated from defence expenditure for this purpose in 1960–61. Of this some £47 million went on basic and applied research, carried out almost entirely by government departments, leaving nearly £190 million for development research. About £175 million of this was spent by way of extra-mural contracts to industry, compared with our estimate above of about £130 million in 1958.

The number of qualified scientists and engineers engaged on defence

[1] Exclusive of undisclosed annual expenditure for defence by the Atomic Energy Authority.

TABLE 13 *Research Expenditure—Industry Breakdown—1958*

Total Expenditure on Research and Development[1]		Cost per qualified worker	Number of qualified workers[5]		Research and Development expenditure as a percentage of the value of net output	
£ million	per cent	£	number	per cent	per cent	
296·7	100·0	10,791	26,225	3·8	All manufacturing industries
196·7	66·3	7,968	22,977	2·6	All manufacturing industries except aircraft
3·2	1·1	8,727	343	1·1	Ceramics, glass, cement etc.
43·04	14·5	6,655	6,368	5·9	Chemicals and allied trades
6·8	2·3	9,844	677	n.a.	of which: a. Mineral oil refining
8·1	2·7	6,923	975	1·15	Metal manufacture
5·1	1·7	6,103	640	0·9	of which: a. Iron and steel
3·0	1·0	8,489	335	2·1	b. Non-ferrous metals
29·4	9·9	8,472	3,307	1·86	Non-electrical engineering and shipbuilding[2]
64·5	21·7	7,472	7,677	9·86	Electrical engineering and electrical goods[3]
24·6	8·3	7,908	2,996	11·9	of which: a. Electronics
100·0	33·7	30,763	3,284	35·7	Aircraft
17·1	5·8	19,778	806	3·3	Motor and other vehicles and accessories
11·6	3·9	13,535	853	10·7	Precision Instruments etc.
8·6	2·9	8,191	939	0·9	Textiles, leather, leather goods and clothing
0·5	0·2	4,804	48	n.a.	of which: a. Cotton
6·6	2·2	10,943	575	n.a.	b. Man-made fibres
5·04	1·7	6,642	705	0·6	Food, drink and tobacco
2·0	0·7	7,244	241	0·25	Manufactures of wood and paper, and printing
4·1	1·4	5,313	763	1·8	Other manufacturing

[1] Includes provisions for depreciation and payments to outside bodies.
[2] Includes metal goods not elsewhere specified.
[3] Includes some mechanical engineering associated with electrical engineering where research and production in both fields are carried out in the same establishment.
[4] Some research on food products is unavoidably included in Chemicals and allied trades.
[5] In establishments with over 100 employees.
* Estimate.
Source: 'Industrial research and development expenditure, 1958', the Department of Scientific and Industrial Research.

work at January, 1959 was estimated at about 20,000 in a report entitled 'Scientific and Engineering Manpower in Great Britain', 1959 (Cmnd. 902). About half of these were engaged on research and they accounted for about one-quarter of all scientists and engineers engaged on research in industry and government establishments. This was a reduction compared with three years earlier when defence accounted for some two-fifths of the qualified personnel engaged on research work. Direct government employment on defence research in 1959 accounted for 3,750 qualified scientists and engineers, leaving some 6,250 in industry out of a total of 26,225 (see Table 13)—or nearly 24 per cent. More recent figures of employment of qualified personnel on research are not available, but it seems probable that in total they have been declining slightly. The Federation of British Industries' survey of 'Industrial Research in Manufacturing Industry, 1959–60', for example, estimated the numbers of qualified scientists and engineers on defence research in manufacturing industry at about 5,500. This was a little under 20 per cent of the total employment of qualified personnel on research, compared with a peak of 30 per cent in the previous five years.

It was not possible to obtain much supplementary information about the impact of defence expenditure on research, since for reasons of security it was laid down that the information obtained on this subject be confined to the replies received to question five of the questionnaire (see Appendix B), relating to the proportion of company research financed by defence contracts. Answers to this question were given by 140 companies and, of these, 62 or 44·3 per cent received no defence contributions to research. The full analysis of the results is given in Table 14, page 31. Only seven companies obtained between 76 and 100 per cent of their total research outlays from defence contracts, compared with 45 that received 10 per cent or less from this source. Of the total of 140 companies, therefore, 107 or 76·4 per cent received either no contribution at all or only up to one-tenth of their total spending on research from defence expenditure. Reliance on defence expenditure for research purposes to any significant extent was mainly confined to the larger companies, as perhaps would be expected.

In total, however, defence expenditure is almost certainly the largest single source of funds for research undertaken in the United Kingdom, and its impact is the greater for being concentrated in relatively few fields. Moreover, whereas in the past there has been a shortage of qualified scientists and technicians, this is not expected to continue, so the ending of defence research contracts could lead to unemployment if

TABLE 14 *The Proportion of Company Research and Development Expenditure Financed by Defence Contracts*

Number of companies in each category

	Proportion of Research and Development Expenditure Financed by Defence Contracts							
Size of companies	nil	Up to 10 per cent	11–25 per cent	26–50 per cent	51–75 per cent	76–100 per cent	Total number of companies	
Companies employing:—								
Up to 100 persons	6	2	nil	nil	nil	nil	8	
101–200	5	3	2	1	1	nil	12	
201–300	7	3	nil	1	nil	nil	11	
301–400	4	1	1	nil	1	nil	7	
401–500	8	3	nil	nil	nil	1	12	
501–750	4	5	nil	nil	nil	nil	9	
751–1,000	4	2	1	1	1	nil	9	
1,001–2,000	8	7	2	nil	2	nil	19	
2,001–3,000	3	4	2	nil	1	1	11	
3,001–4,000	2	3	nil	nil	nil	2	7	
4,001–5,000	2	1	nil	nil	nil	nil	3	
5,001–10,000	8	4	nil	nil	2	2	16	
More than 10,000 persons	1	7	2	4	1	1	16	
Total all Companies	62	45	10	7	9	7	140	
Percentage Breakdown	44·3	32·1	7·1	5·0	6·4	5·0	100	

not replaced by civil expenditure of similar proportions. The report on 'The Long-Term Demand for Scientific Manpower', 1961 (Cmnd. 1490), concluded that 'the overall supply and demand for qualified man-power will not be very much out of balance at the end of the first five years of the decade 1960/70'. This conclusion was subject to a number of assumptions and reservations, but there seems little doubt that this view would have been put forward more strongly if disarmament had been considered probable. In fact, it was assumed that total outlays on defence would be broadly the same in 1970 as in 1959, but that the proportion devoted to research could be somewhat higher.

There are two problems likely to be faced in the event of disarmament putting an end to defence expenditure on research. First, unless the projects concerned are replaced by similar ones financed by government civil expenditure, there is likely to be considerable unemployment amongst the workers concerned in the short term. Figures of government employment on defence research are not published in full, partly for security reasons, and up-to-date estimates are not available for private industry. Leaving aside nuclear research, however, it is probable that the number of qualified workers involved lies between 8,000 and 10,000. This does not reflect the full amount of unemployment that would result since a considerable number of unqualified workers are also involved. The D.S.I.R. enquiry, for example, showed that in manufacturing industry at January 1959 the 26,225 qualified workers in research were supplemented by a further 87,283 lower or non-qualified persons—a ratio of over 3 : 1. If this ratio holds true for defence research, then total employment is likely to be in the region of 40,000. The likely effects for separate industries and government employees are considered in greater detail in the following sections.

The second and less calculable effect depends on the stimulus that defence research gives to advances in the civil field. In the United Kingdom in 1958–59 total research expenditure accounted for 2·3 per cent of the gross national product compared with 2·7 per cent in the United States, and it is often argued that the higher proportion in America, coupled with the much larger sums involved, gives the United States a competitive advantage in a number of non-defence fields. A large military bomber can be converted into a civil airliner for a relatively low development charge compared with the sums involved in producing a new civil airliner from scratch, an example being the Boeing 707 airliner which was developed from the Boeing bomber. Many similar though less obvious examples could be found in the field of electronics. If defence research is not replaced by a comparable amount of civil expenditure some of the country's impetus to growth is likely to be lost. Private industry has increased its research outlays quite sharply in recent years, but it clearly could not find another £175 million at short notice, particularly when the industries most vitally concerned are likely to be depressed. The need to consider the alternative provision of funds for research will, therefore, be considered in greater detail in Part 2 of this study.

Chapter 5

The Balance of Payments

Military expenditure constitutes a significant burden on the balance of payments, as expenditure is considerably in excess of receipts. Moreover, the overall deficit on military account has widened quite sharply in recent years, as can be seen from the following table taken from the official balance of payments statistics.

TABLE 15 *The Balance of Military Expenditure and Receipts on Government Account*

£ million			
1959	1960	1961	Expenditure:
115	133	137	Rest of Sterling Area
54	76	90	Non-Sterling Area
169	209	227	Total
			Receipts:
10	10	8	Rest of Sterling Area
18	20	18	U.S. and Canadian Forces' Expenditure
11	14	14	Other Non-Sterling Areas
39	44	40	Total
130	163	187	Net Deficit

Source: United Kingdom Balance of Payments 1959 to 1961. Cmnd. 1671.

A major cause of concern in recent years was the growing cost, in terms of foreign exchange, of maintaining British troops on the Continent—particularly in West Germany. The position was aggravated by the ending of the three year Anglo-German Agreement at the end of 1960, under which West Germany previously made an annual contribution of £12 million to the cost of maintaining British troops in that country. Following the sterling crisis in mid-1961 and the measures taken in July, the United Kingdom asked for assistance from its N.A.T.O. allies towards the cost of maintaining British troops stationed in western Europe. The validity of this request was recognised by the countries concerned, and after lengthy negotiations the West German Government agreed in March, 1962 to make purchases of DM.600 million (£54 million) in this country, over and above the normal United Kingdom exports, to help meet the costs of the British Army of the Rhine. This compares with the current annual cost of maintaining troops in West Germany of £73 million, and goes most of the way to ease the current burden.

A further offsetting factor is the trade balance on sales of arms, which is only partly reflected in the balance of payments figures. It is not possible to assess this with any accuracy, but it seems clear that it has declined in recent years.[1] Demand fell as countries completed their rearmament programmes in the mid-1950's, whilst competition for orders increased. With the exception of any special agreements that may be negotiated, therefore, the contribution from sales of armaments is not expected to be very important in the future.

Outpayments to countries in the rest of the sterling area are not likely to change significantly in the immediate future, though a greater reliance on mobile reserves based in the United Kingdom may tend to reduce them in the longer run, or at least prevent them from increasing. Disarmament would, therefore, lead to a considerable easing on the United Kingdom's balance of payments in this respect, although this would be partially offset by a corresponding worsening of the balance of the rest of the sterling area as a whole. To some extent military expenditure of this nature can be considered as a form of aid to underdeveloped regions, although since the position of military bases depends upon strategic and not economic considerations, it is unlikely to be distributed to the best advantage. Some saving in payments to the more prosperous areas should be possible, but the main effect of disarmament in the short run would almost certainly have to be the transfer of military outpayments to direct economic aid.

---

[1] In 1960, United Kingdom exports of arms, ammunition and military stores (partly included in off-shore sales to the United States government) totalled £30 million, compared with £56 million in 1955.

The wider economic implications of disarmament in the international sphere can only be touched upon in this study. The general easing of tension which would accompany a universal disarmament agreement should lead to an expansion in world trade, despite the cessation of trade in armaments as such, since it should make possible the removal of restrictions to trade based on defence considerations. For example, trade between the east and west is restricted to non-strategic materials in a number of instances, and even when there are no strategic considerations involved the fear of becoming too dependent on a possibly hostile source of supply often overrides the normal commercial criteria.

The effect that disarmament would have on the demand for particular raw materials entering international trade is not thought likely to be very significant. This conclusion is based on a United States survey, the results of which were summarised in the recent United Nations' Report on the 'Economic and Social Consequences of Disarmament' discussed earlier. As a result of this study and certain assumptions about the use made of released resources in the event of disarmament, the United Nations' experts concluded that the effect on the demand for primary products currently used in quantity for defence purposes would be marginal. However, they pointed out that in current supply-demand conditions, minor changes in demand for particular products can lead to considerable price swings which would adversely affect the export earnings of primary producers—mainly under-developed countries. The possible impact of such changes can be seen from the following quotation:—

> 'For example, a 6 per cent drop in their average export prices, were it to take place, would imply for the under-developed countries a decline in their foreign exchange earnings equivalent to something like one-half of all official economic grants and loans currently received from abroad in a year.'

Price changes of this order are not peculiar to disarmament, however, as they can and do occur as a result of any general decline in world industrial activity. The best way to prevent them happening in the event of disarmament would be to ensure by national policies that there was no check to economic growth in the major industrial countries of the world. To the extent that this is not possible in the short run, the case for using some of the released resources to provide aid to the under-developed countries is strengthened.

PART ONE

2. *Defence and Industry*

Chapter 6

The Sectors Likely to be Affected

In the previous chapters a study was made of the impact of defence expenditure on broad sectors of the economy. Since it has been assumed that the government of the day would take steps to keep any dislocation resulting from disarmament to a minimum, particularly as regards the level of employment, it is also necessary to study some individual sectors of the economy in greater detail in order to see whether they are likely to need special assistance if defence expenditure ends.

One such sector is the armed services. In the event of disarmament it is to be expected that all but a very small proportion of the personnel of the armed forces would return to civil life. Recent developments have, however, given a foretaste of the problems likely to be involved, and for the most part they provide an encouraging picture. Changes in defence policy which were set out in the Statement on Defence, 1957, resulted in a substantial reduction in the size of the services and an end to the system of National Service. Considerable experience has been gained, therefore, in the resettlement under present day conditions of large numbers of Service personnel suddenly dismissed from the Forces, particularly of officers, where the problems involved have proved more difficult to overcome.

The numbers would, of course, be much greater in the event of disarmament and the problems could well prove more intractable if conditions in outside industry and commerce were depressed. Nevertheless, it seems reasonable to assume that the process of demobilisation would be spread over at least one year, and almost certainly much longer, so that the numbers involved at any one time would not be unmanageable. The cost of a resettlement and training scheme, plus the payment of gratuities to ex-Service men, may well average about £1,000 per head, so that some £400–450 million would be involved—the major part of which is likely to be spent over a period of two years.

The probable extent of redundancy and unemployment in the

service and supply departments in the event of disarmament is more difficult to estimate. As was seen earlier, because government production and research workers are included with workers in private industry in the official figures, it is necessary to exclude them when considering the civil service in order to avoid double counting. This leaves some 200,000 persons, the largest single group of whom are employed mainly at the respective Ministry headquarters in London.

Many of these would, of course, be required in the early stages of any disarmament scheme to administer the run-down of the armed forces and the numerous defence projects in progress at that time. During this period, which would probably take a minimum of two years, growing numbers of civil servants would become redundant, many of whom could probably be absorbed into civil departments which may well expand if defence expenditure ceases. In addition, it should prove possible to place the lower grades of clerical workers for whom there are no vacancies in civil departments in non-government posts, since there is a general shortage of this type of labour (particularly in the London area), after payment of suitable compensation for loss of any pension rights or other special privileges. Probably the greatest difficulty would be faced in the case of senior civil servants for whom no alternative posts could be found. These are unlikely to be large in number; they should not exceed 10,000 persons, and the payment of full retirement pensions in the event of their early dismissal might well prove to be the most advantageous and equitable way of dealing with the persons concerned. In total, however, the problem should not prove a major one, as after allowing for normal wastage and the opportunities for further employment that would exist, at the most some 50,000 persons, or one-quarter of the total, would probably be involved.

It is much more difficult to assess the extent of the problems likely to be faced by individual industries and firms in the event of disarmament, and the remainder of this section is, therefore, devoted to a number of industry studies. The industries investigated are those known to carry out most of the defence contracts let to private industry, though they also include the government employees engaged on similar work. It is, therefore, of interest to see first how many and what type of government employees are concerned, since they may well constitute a special problem in the event of disarmament.

These persons are, for the most part, employed in Royal Ordnance Factories, Admiralty dockyards and government research establishments, though some may also be employed at service establishments. When considering the figures, however, it should be borne in mind that the persons concerned are also included in the appropriate employment figures in the individual industry analyses (after making an allowance for any differences in timing), and that, for the most part, they do not constitute an additional problem. However, whereas in private industry it is possible, and in many instances already the case, that private firms can undertake new lines of business, this is not true of government concerns. Unless, therefore, the government decides to enter the field of general manufacturing industry, workers in government establishments are likely to face special problems in the event of disarmament, and it is for this reason they are considered separately.

The employment figures supplied by the Ministry of Aviation and the service departments relate to the position during the period October, 1961 to May, 1962, but can broadly be taken as indicative of the position during the first quarter of 1962.

In total, the departments employed 162,115 industrial workers of all types, of whom 60,659 were skilled and 101,456 unskilled. These figures include research and inspectorate personnel in addition to production workers, as well as the industrial worker grades employed at Service establishments. Full details of the areas in the country in which these workers were employed are not available, but a clear idea of the area pattern of employment can be obtained from the following table, which relates to industrial civil servants employed by the Ministry of Aviation, the War Office (excluding inspectorate employees) and the Admiralty.

It can be seen from Table 16 that the regions most concerned are London and the south east, the southern and eastern combined and the south-western, with skilled workers in particular being concentrated in these regions. The London and south-eastern and the eastern and southern regions combined are both areas of below average unemployment, where vacancies in the main skilled occupations exceed the numbers of unemployed by a high margin. Unemployment is currently slightly higher in the south-western region, but still a little below the national average rate, and although the demand for labour in that region is more closely matched to the supply no serious difficulties over the re-employment of industrial civil servants seems likely. Of greater significance is the relatively high level of employment in Scotland where unemployment is currently well above the national average rate, and government workers in this area might well need special assistance.

TABLE 16 *The Area Pattern of Employment of Industrial Civil Servants Engaged on Defence Work*

	Skilled Workers		Unskilled Workers		Total	
	number[1]	percent of Total	number[1]	percent of Total	number[1]	percent of Total
London and South-Eastern	7,216·5	17·7	12,350·0	16·1	19,566·5	16·6
Southern and Eastern	12,274·0	29·9	18,036·0	23·5	30,310·0	25·8
South-Western	10,393·0	25·3	18,540·0	24·2	28,933·0	24·6
Midlands	1,305·0	3·2	2,944·5	3·8	4,249·5	3·6
North-Midland	746·0	1·8	929·0	1·2	1,675·0	1·4
East and West Ridings	436·0	1·1	534·0	0·7	970·0	0·8
North-Western	1499·0	3·7	5,682·0	7·4	7,181·0	6·1
Northern	383·0	0·9	2,123·0	2·8	2,506·0	2·1
Wales	1,207·0	2·9	3,730·5	4·9	4,937·5	4·2
Scotland	4,759·0	11·6	10,782·0	14·1	15,541·0	13·2
Northern Ireland	787·0	1·9	963·0	1·3	1,750·0	1·5
	41,005·5	100·0	76,614·0	100·0	117,619·5	100·0

[1] Part time workers are classed as half a full time worker (0·5).

Source: Ministry of Aviation, War Office and the Admiralty.

Details were also given of the numbers of qualified scientists and engineers employed by the service and supply departments on defence work. These totalled 6,505 persons, the vast majority of whom appear to be employed in England and Wales. A detailed breakdown by region is not available. Only in the case of the Ministry of Aviation and the Admiralty were the figures subdivided into those engaged on research and development, those engaged on production and those engaged on management and similar duties: the proportions were 58·7 per cent, 23·6 per cent and 17·8 per cent respectively. In the light of current estimates about the balance of demand for qualified persons engaged on research work, it seems probable that special measures would be needed to ensure that a proportion of these workers was not unemployed as a result of disarmament. In the short term this could probably be achieved most cheaply if they were employed on civil research under the auspices of the Department of Scientific and Industrial Research, if this were politically possible.

The separate industry analyses which follow are in four sections. The first three deal with aircraft, electronics and shipbuilding—the three major defence industries—while the fourth covers the industries which are less dependent on defence expenditure. Separate conclusions have been given at the end of each section, and when considering these in respect of the level of unemployment which could result from disarmament, it is useful to do so in the context of the general manpower situation. Much valuable information on this subject was contained in a recent report, published in the Ministry of Labour Gazette, February 1962, by the working party on the manpower situation set up by the National Joint Advisory Council.

This report emphasised the shortage of skilled labour and pointed out that 'Except for brief periods of recession, there has been a shortage of workers in most skilled occupations since the end of the war.' The ways in which this shortage has affected particular industries and regions can be seen from the following extract:

'Some idea of the extent of this shortage may be obtained by comparing the number of workers wholly unemployed in different skilled occupations with the number of unfilled vacancies notified to employment exchanges. There may be a tendency on the part of some employers to inflate their demands for skilled labour in the hope of obtaining at least a few men, but, equally, there is a tendency (deriving from the knowledge that the skilled labour needed is virtually unobtainable) not to notify all vacancies to the

Ministry. On balance, it seems more likely that the ratio of wholly unemployed to vacancies notified understates the actual shortage.

There was, in September 1961, an excess of unfilled vacancies over unemployed in nearly all the main skilled trades, making an apparent shortage of over 30,000 workers, including about 20,000 engineering craftsmen and 10,000 building craftsmen. In a wide range of skilled engineering and allied trades taken together, the number of outstanding vacancies was three-and-a-half times the number of men unemployed. There were particularly acute shortages of turners, machine tool setters, instrument makers and draughtsmen. The shortage was least acute in the trades associated with shipbuilding and shiprepairing, and this reflects the current difficulties of those industries, but even here in certain trades, the number of vacancies exceeded unemployment over the country as a whole. Among building craftsmen, there were over four vacancies to every man unemployed, with particularly acute shortages of bricklayers, carpenters and joiners.

The extent of the shortage varies considerably between regions. In September 1961, the shortages were generally most acute in the south and east of England, the midlands and Yorkshire. However, there was a clear excess of vacancies over unemployed in all regions except Scotland, where the position was affected by the difficulties of the shipbuilding industry. Skilled labour is difficult to obtain even in many development districts.

The shortage of skilled workers has not only varied with the general employment situation but has also shown broadly the same seasonal variations as unemployment in general, being greatest in summer and least in winter. The figures for September 1961 are close to the average for the last five or six years, and given the continuance of a high level of economic activity, it is reasonable to expect a persistence of the same degree of shortage unless the supply of skilled workers is increased.

It is significant that the main shortages of skilled workers are in building and engineering occupations. Since the building and engineering industries are of basic importance to the economy, the effects of shortages of skilled manpower extend far beyond these particular industries. Further, as roughly one-third of the workers in these occupations are employed in industries other than building and engineering, shortages are felt directly over wide fields of employment.'

Because the shortage was expected to persist the report went on to consider ways in which it might be alleviated. One suggestion, that facilities for retraining workers should be more widely used and that conditions of eligibility and suitability be extended, seems very pertinent to the problems likely to arise in the event of disarmament. The opening of government training centres to ex-servicemen and industrial workers who lose their jobs because of the ending of defence expenditure, with a guaranteed income during the retraining period, could be of considerable value in mitigating the human problems likely to be involved in the conversion to an entirely non-defence economy.

Chapter 7

The Aircraft Industry

SIZE AND STRUCTURE OF THE INDUSTRY

The value of total production[1] by the aircraft industry has changed very little since 1956. It showed a slight fall in 1960 at an estimated £415 million, but recovered to £435 million in 1961. This figure includes the manufacture and repair of airframes and aero-engines, the manufacture of parts and accessories other than electrical or electronic equipment, that part of the production of guided missiles which can be attributed to the aircraft rather than to the electronics industry, and research and development carried out on behalf of the government.

Production records have varied between the different sectors of the industry. This is shown most clearly by the export figures, which are a useful measure of the state of the aircraft industry, since the domestic market alone is normally insufficient to cover development costs. The decline in exports of complete aircraft has been marked, and they are expected to fall once more in 1962. Exports of aero-engines, on the other hand, have continued to rise, as have exports of parts.

The troubles of the aircraft industry have partly been caused by the continued trend towards larger and more complex aircraft, resulting in ever increasing development costs. By 1958 the aircraft industry was spending the equivalent of nearly 36 per cent of net output on research

[1] The value of the production of an industry can vary widely according to the definition used. For this survey a definition was required for the major industries investigated that permits of direct comparison with defence expenditure; this is known as the 'ring fence' concept of production.Broadly, it defines an industry's output as its sales to final buyers. It omits all inter firm transactions within the industry but includes the value of all 'bought-in' materials and components. The figure obtained by using this definition tends to lie roughly half way between the values of net and gross output, and for this reason the results may differ from those in other surveys. It was felt, however, that the advantage of being able to compare defence expenditure directly with the value of production outweighed any disadvantages due to unfamiliarity.

Exports by the U K. Aircraft Industry

£ million

	Complete new aircraft	New engines	Used aircraft and engines; parts etc.	Total
1956	49·4	7·6	45·2	102·2
1957	46·0	9·9	57·8	113·7
1958	71·2	19·2	61·0	151·4
1959	60·5	25·5	68·7	154·7
1960	37·6	30·7	72·6	140·9
1961	35·0[1]	33·2	78·0[1]	146·6

Preliminary figure.
Source: Treasury Bulletin for Industry, September 1961.

and development, as compared to an average of under 4 per cent of net output for all manufacturing industry.[1] This factor, together with the prospect after 1957 of a decline in orders for military aircraft, led to government insistence on a widespread rationalisation of the aircraft industry into a few large units. Reorganisation began at the end of 1959, as a result of which the industry now consists of three main airframe groups and two main aero-engine groups. Only three major companies remain outside these groups.

This reorganisation has gone some way towards solving the industry's problems, although there is still considerable scope for further rationalisation, particularly on the design side. Employment in the aircraft industry in Great Britain stood at 298,100 in May, 1961. The industry has substantial work in hand, but orders for new projects are low. The approaching completion of large military contracts has resulted recently in the announcement of the closing down, in the near future, of three separate plants, and of reductions at others, involving the redundancy of a total of 10,000 workers, and further cuts in capacity can be expected.

The industry is currently in a transitional phase both on the civil and on the military side. On the civil side orders for the last generation of jets and turbo-prop airliners are approaching completion, while the next generation of jets is still in the development stage. Sufficient orders for these have not yet been placed, and cannot in any case affect production until 1963 or 1964. On the military side, although the value of orders has been maintained, fewer types and fewer aircraft are required,

[1] Department of Scientific and Industrial Research. 'Industrial Research and Development Expenditure.' 1958.

and military export markets are also smaller. Competition in both civil and military export markets, particularly from the American industry, is intensifying.

Some permanent reduction in capacity can be expected in the aircraft industry over the next few years, a figure as high as 25 per cent having been suggested by some observers, and the immediate market outlook is not favourable even if there is no reduction in total defence expenditure. The industry has some good long term prospects, however, notably in vertical-take-off fighters, in civil supersonic aircraft, and in small executive aircraft. A government design contract has also recently been placed for a variable geometry aircraft. A trend towards international co-operation over these new projects has emerged both on the military and on the civil side, and this should result in a reduction in capital costs, although it will do little to solve the problem of excess capacity.

THE AIRCRAFT INDUSTRY AND DEFENCE SPENDING

Government spending on the aircraft industry was stated in March 1962 to be running at the level of about £300 million a year. This total consists almost entirely of spending for defence purposes, including purchases of aircraft and guided missiles for the three services, and expenditure on research and development on military aircraft and guided missiles carried out within the industry. It excludes the majority of government contributions to civil aircraft development.

The total of £300 million can be broken down to some extent according to information given in the Defence Estimates.

Items from the Defence Estimates Showing Spending on the Aircraft Industry

£million 1960/61	1961/62	
		Air Estimates[1]:
80·4	91·2	a. Airframes, spares, components, accessories etc.
51·4	58·7	b. Aero-engines, spares, components, accessories etc.
1·6	3·5	Army Estimates: Aircraft
38·7	33·3	Navy Estimates: Aircraft, including repairs
172·1	186·7	

[1] Revised estimates.

In addition to these items a small proportion of spending on aircraft equipment, also listed in the air estimates, should probably be attributed to the aircraft industry rather than to engineering and electronics firms. Spending on guided missiles is included in all three service estimates under a general armaments total which cannot be broken down, and contributions to research and development in the aircraft industry, which are made by the Ministry of Aviation, are also given under general totals in the civil estimates. Research and development expenditure has, however, been estimated as being in the region of £100 million. This includes some of the Ministry's contributions to research on civil projects, but as these are supported largely as a result of their military applications, the total can be justifiably attributed to defence expenditure.

The total defence expenditure of £300 million should probably be reduced slightly for the calendar year 1961 in order to compare it with the estimate of total output by the industry of £435 million. Nevertheless it seems unlikely that the proportion of the aircraft industry's total output represented by defence markets was less than 65 per cent, and it was more probably nearer to 70 per cent. This percentage would be only slightly reduced if defence expenditure exclusive of the estimate for research and development were taken as a proportion of total output exclusive of research and development work for the government. It would not be significantly increased by the addition of exports of military aircraft, the share of these in total exports having declined rapidly in recent years to a very low level.

The importance of defence spending to the aircraft industry is less apparent from the employment figures. The number employed on defence work in aircraft manufacture and repair in May, 1961 was 136,900. This was just under 46 per cent of the total employed in the industry. The difference between this percentage and the percentage attributable to defence illustrates the high proportion of defence expenditure going to research and development rather than to production.

Total research and development expenditure by the aircraft industry in 1961 is estimated at £125 million.[1] The proportion contributed by defence was in the region of 80 per cent. This does not include the cost of work carried out at government research establishments, which is

---

[1] This would amount to just under 30 per cent of production. This figure cannot be compared with that given by the D.S.I.R. for 1958, where the calculation was based on net output.

also excluded from the industry total. A similar estimate of the proportion of research and development financed by defence in the American aircraft industry amounted to 86 per cent in 1959.

RESULTS OF THE QUESTIONNAIRES

Eight questionnaires were returned by the aircraft industry, covering a total of ten airframe manufacturers and six aero-engine manufacturers. All but one of the respondents made other products besides aircraft for defence purposes. Four were manufacturers of guided weapons or of engines for guided weapons, two of vehicle engines and three of electronic equipment. The total number employed by these companies was 223,850, of which 50 per cent were wholly (or mostly) engaged on defence work. It is evident that neither these figures nor those that follow can be taken as strictly representative of the relationship between aircraft production and defence spending, both as a result of the bias of the questionnaires returned and because of the overlap into other manufacturing sectors.

Questionnaires were also returned by 42 firms manufacturing aircraft equipment for defence purposes, of which 24 also produced naval or military equipment. Types of product included were electrical and electronic equipment for aircraft and guided weapons, ground equipment for aerodromes, aircraft simulators, and equipment and components used in the manufacture of aircraft and missiles. The total number employed by these firms was 200,066, of which approximately 12 per cent were employed wholly (or mostly) on defence work.

The questionnaires relating to aircraft manufacture can be divided into two groups, one consisting of five returns each covering up to 25,000 employees, and the other consisting of three returns each covering over 50,000 employees. The five smaller manufacturing units are all considerably more heavily involved in defence work, both as a percentage of turnover and as a percentage of expenditure on research and development, than the three larger groups. The lowest percentage of turnover attributed to defence contracts by any of the eight was 20 per cent.

The heavy dependence of aircraft manufacturers on defence work is indicated by both Table 17 and Table 18. Table 19 shows the regional distribution of branches of the respondent firms carrying out defence work. Aircraft manufacture for defence appears from this to be fairly widely distributed over the country, but official statistics (as shown in the table on page 14) indicate that the greatest concentration is in fact in the north western, south western, and eastern and southern regions.

TABLE 17 *Aircraft Manufacturers; Percentage of Turnover Attributable to Defence Contracts*

Number of returns

Up to 10%	11–25%	26–50%	51–75%	76–100%	Total Number of Returns	Companies employing
nil	nil	nil	nil	5	5	Up to 25,000
nil	1	1	1	nil	3	50,000 and over

TABLE 18 *Aircraft Manufacturers; Percentage of Research and Development Financed by Defence*

Number of returns

Up to 10%	11–25%	26–50%	51–75%	76–100%	Total Number of Returns	Companies employing
nil	nil	nil	1	4	5	Up to 25,000
nil	nil	1	1	nil	2[1]	50,000 and over

[1] Information was not available for the third company.

TABLE 19 *Aircraft Manufacturers; Regional Distribution of Factories with Defence Work*

North	E. & W. Ridings	North Midland	East	London & S.E.	South	Companies employing
1	nil	nil	1	2	1	Up to 25,000
nil	3	3	nil	2	1	50,000 and over
1	3	3	1	4	2	Total all Companies

South West	Wales	Midland	North West	Scotland	N. Ireland	
2	nil	2	nil	nil	1	Up to 25,000
1	1	1	1	1	nil	50,000 and over
3	1	3	1	1	1	Total all Companies

The last two questions in the questionnaire related to the situation that would be likely to arise if disarmament were to take place. The opinions expressed by aircraft manufacturers showed little variation from company to company. Two of the respondents, both employing under 10,000 workers, said that resources were theoretically fully transferable to civil work; the remaining six respondents said that resources were partially transferable, one of these specifying some research and development equipment as being non-transferable. The possibility of the transfer of resources does not of course imply that it will take place, since an equally important question is whether civil markets will be available for the output involved. The main problems expected to arise were those of redundancy and how to find alternative work; the three largest groups saw redundancy as inevitable in any circumstances, and two others saw it as inevitable unless a very long period of warning were given. Even if alternative work existed, civil markets would be unable to bear the costs of research and development, and the problem of time and finance for adaptation was also mentioned.

Manufacturers of aircraft equipment appeared considerably less dependent on defence work.

TABLE 20 *Manufacturers of Aircraft Equipment; Percentage of Turnover Attributable to Defence Contracts*

Number of returns

Up to 10%	11–25%	26–50%	51–75%	76–100%	Total Number of Returns	Companies employing
2	1	2	1	1	7	Up to 200
7	1	3	4	1	16	201–1,000
11	1	4	2	1	19	Over 1,000
20	3	9	7	3	42	Total all Companies

Just under half of the 42 respondents were not involved in defence work by more than 10 per cent of their turnover. The majority of the remaining half tended to be fairly heavily involved in defence work, in nearly all cases by at least 26 per cent of turnover; just under 25 per cent of all companies were involved by more than 50 per cent of turnover. A larger proportion of the small and medium-sized companies was heavily dependent on defence work than was the case with the large companies.

There was still less dependence on defence contributions to research and development expenditure. Well over half of all companies either received no contributions from defence or a sum amounting to less than 10 per cent of their total research and development expenditure, while the proportion receiving more than 50 per cent of total expenditure was under 17 per cent. There was no apparent difference between large and medium-sized companies as to the degree of dependence on defence contributions.

TABLE 21 *Manufacturers of Aircraft Equipment; Percentage of Research and Development Financed by Defence*

Number of returns

nil	Up to 10%	11–25%	26–50%	51–75%	76–100%	Total Number of Returns	Companies employing
3	1	1	1	1	nil	7	Up to 200
6	5	nil	3	1	1	16	201–1,000
6	6	1	2	2	2	19	Over 1,000
15	12	2	6	4	3	42	Total all Companies

The questionnaires showed a heavy concentration of defence work on aircraft equipment in the London and south-eastern region and in the midlands. This corresponds to a certain extent with the area breakdown of the official employment figures, although for aircraft manufacturing and repairing as a whole the main concentration of defence work is in the north western, south western, and eastern and southern regions.

TABLE 22 *Manufacturers of Aircraft Equipment; Regional Distribution of Factories with Defence Work*

North	E. & W. Ridings	North Midland	East	London & S.E.	South	Companies employing
nil	nil	nil	nil	3	1	Up to 200
1	nil	1	nil	7	1	201–1,000
2	2	3	2	10	3	Over 1,000
3	2	4	2	20	5	Total all Companies

South West	Wales	Midland	North West	Scotland	N. Ireland	
nil	nil	2	1	nil	nil	Up to 200
nil	nil	6	2	nil	nil	201–1,000
2	3	8	5	2	1	Over 1,000
2	3	16	8	2	1	Total all Companies

Nearly three-quarters of all manufacturers believed that resources could be fully transferred to civil production. Half of the small firms and just under a third of the large firms replying to this question felt that resources could be only partially transferred. The medium-sized firms appeared to be the least likely to be affected by redundancy of resources.

TABLE 23 *Manufacturers of Aircraft Equipment; how far Production Resources could be Transferred to Civil Work*

Number of returns

Entirely	Partially	Not at all	Companies employing
2	3	1	Up to 200
14	1	nil	201–1,000
12	6	1	Over 1,000
28	10	2	Total all Companies

The main problems anticipated by manufacturers of aircraft equipment in the event of disarmament were those of temporary redundancy of part of the labour force while commercial work was being built up, and of obtaining alternative markets. Six companies envisaged permanent redundancy for part of the labour force, and six companies expected that a general industrial decline would have an indirect effect on their markets. Six companies expected no problems at all, but none of these was involved in defence work by more than 10 per cent of turnover.

RESULTS OF THE INTERVIEWS

Interviews were carried out within three airframe groups, covering a total of nine aircraft companies, with two aero-engine manufacturers,

TABLE 24 *Manufacturers of Aircraft Equipment; the Main Problems of Disarmament*

Number of times mentioned

By Companies Employing:—				
Up to 200	201–1,000	over 1,000	Total times mentioned	
I	5	6	12	Temporary redundancy while commercial work is built up
I	5	5	11	Excess capacity—how to find alternative markets
2	I	3	6	Permanent redundancy
nil	2	4	6	Indirect effects of a general fall in demand
I	nil	I	2	How to maintain research expenditure
nil	I	nil	I	Lower profits
I	2	3	6	None

and with thirteen manufacturers of aircraft equipment. The purpose of the interviews was to gather more detailed information on the situation that might be expected if disarmament were to take place; on the problems of the transfer of resources, the expansion of existing civil markets and the opening up of new ones, and the maintenance of research and development facilities. The companies were also asked if they had had any previous experience of cuts in defence contracts, and what sort of government action they would think desirable in order to alleviate the problems caused by disarmament.

Transfer of resources. Airframe manufacturers believed the labour employed in the industry to be largely transferable, either to civil aircraft production or to other manufacturing lines. The mobility of the skilled machinist was said to be limited by region rather than occupation, and engineers and technicians were also said to be normally able to transfer from one line of production to another. The only types of employee mentioned as being difficult to transfer were designers, who were said to have to undergo considerable readjustment in order to conform to normal engineering objectives. The same views were held by the majority of aero-engine and aircraft equipment manufacturers. Two of the latter mentioned a general shortage of skilled technicians, who they believed could readily be absorbed by civil work; two manufacturers of electronic aircraft equipment, however, said that a certain proportion of their most highly skilled workers would need long periods of retraining before they could be transferred to other work. Another manufacturer pointed out that the most highly paid of their skilled workers could only be transferred from defence to civil work within the same company if the latter were equally profitable to the company.

Plant and equipment used in airframe manufacture were said to be less readily transferable. Buildings tend to be too tall for normal manufacturing purposes, involving exceptionally high heating and maintenance costs; there is much specialised machinery which could only be used for civil aircraft production or possibly for a space research programme. Aero-engine manufacture involves a higher proportion of general purpose high precision machinery, which can be transferred within the field of precision engineering, although there are some exceptional items of equipment, particularly for testing purposes, which would be unlikely to find civil use. A similar situation prevailed among the majority of manufacturers of aircraft equipment.

Expansion of civil markets. None of the companies interviewed saw any prospects of expanding production of, or for, civil aircraft as even a partial substitute for defence markets in the years immediately following disarmament. One aircraft manufacturer said that, on the contrary, the civil aircraft industry would collapse without the support of defence expenditure. Several manufacturers, assuming some degree of continued government support to the industry, mentioned a supersonic airliner and vertical-take-off civil aircraft as possible substitute markets in the long run, but it was generally realised that these would make no difference to production lines in present circumstances until at least ten years after disarmament had begun. One aircraft manufacturer and two manufacturers of aircraft equipment were more hopeful about the prospects for small aircraft, and particularly helicopters, for the use of business executives.

Manufacturers of airframes and aero-engines were, as might be expected, considerably more pessimistic about the prospects of expansion into new markets than were manufacturers of aircraft equipment. It was stressed that it was extremely difficult for an aircraft producer to change to some other line of production, particularly without relevant management experience. One manufacturer of aero-engines commented that while it was theoretically possible to transfer the greater part of the company's resources now engaged on defence work to the manufacture of various civil products, such as tractors, mass-production of the most likely products was now necessary in order to reach the market price, so that a large expansion of capital resources would be involved. Another aero-engine manufacturer suggested the possibility of further expansion in the field of peaceful nuclear energy, and a programme of space research was twice mentioned as a possible source of work in the long run.

Manufacturers of aircraft equipment were in any case considerably more diversified than manufacturers of aircraft, and nearly all of those interviewed had some line of civil production not connected with the aircraft industry which they would expect to expand. Manufacturers of electronic aircraft equipment suggested that defence resources could be largely transferred to the production of computers, industrial controls and civil communications systems. One firm of high precision engineers was confident that a large number of civil products would present alternative work in time, suggesting specifically the new types of civil aircraft, helicopters for business purposes, marine nuclear engineering, and components for computers and industrial controls. Another firm with a very similar production range, however, said that they would find great difficulty in finding markets outside the aircraft industry, and companies manufacturing ground handling and servicing equipment for aircraft were also worried, although they suggested that new civil markets might be found in electro-hydraulics and particularly in earth-moving equipment.

Previous experience of cuts in defence spending. Previous experience of cuts in defence contracts were quoted by a number of manufacturers of aircraft equipment, but less frequently by manufacturers within the aircraft industry proper. One aero-engine company had attempted to diversify in 1945, but had found production in a new sector of industry very unrewarding and had abandoned the project. As a result, they had cut their total labour force by 50 per cent over five years and now felt that a policy of reduction was better than one of diversification. Another aero-engine company had made efforts towards diversification into textile and printing machinery in recent years, in anticipation of contraction in the aircraft industry, but had found themselves uncompetitive in these markets.

Four manufacturers of aircraft equipment had suffered from delays or cuts in defence contracts, which in three cases had resulted in redundancies, and three manufacturers had always tried to diversify as much as possible in order to avoid this eventuality. One company quoted the reverse experience of a subsidiary, which had lost contracts for the manufacture of parts for nuclear power stations. In this case designers and technicians had been successfully transferred to the aircraft industry.

What sort of government action would be needed on disarmament? The effects of disarmament on the aircraft industry would be so momentous that several of the companies interviewed which were wholly or largely engaged in aircraft work could hardly begin to consider what government action could be taken in the circumstances. This was particularly true of the airframe manufacturers. One large airframe manufacturer suggested that a government space research programme could be started, and that financial assistance could be given towards the re-training of skilled employees, but did not feel that these actions would go far towards solving the problems that would arise. A manufacturer of smaller aircraft was rather more optimistic, and proposed the encouragement of an aircraft export drive through a more generous system of export credits, and government assistance towards reducing prices for sales in certain countries along the lines said to be followed by the American and French governments. This manufacturer also felt that at least two years' warning should be given before defence contracts were withdrawn, and that a continued subsidy to research and development would be necessary.

Both aero-engine manufacturers felt that government help should not be given directly to individual firms, but preferably to badly hit regions or through such indirect means as spending on the railways and hospitals, or through government orders, open to competitive tender, for ocean liners, new types of civil aircraft, and other projects which might be selected by the National Research and Development Council. Aid to the under-developed countries would, it was thought, also ultimately result in work for British manufacturers.

Aid to under-developed countries was also mentioned by three manufacturers of aircraft equipment, one of whom suggested that the Government should buy aircraft for lease to these countries at low rents. Two manufacturers thought that there would have to be an interim period of up to three years, either of warning that defence contracts were going to end after that time, or of large-scale aid to heavily involved firms, and a period of warning was mentioned by several others. Five other manufacturers believed that financial aid for re-tooling should be given to individual firms, and six thought that some form of assistance to research and development would be essential. There were various suggestions as to which markets could be enlarged or created by government contracts or systems of tax reliefs; industrial automation, the new types of civil aircraft, and a peaceful nuclear power programme were all mentioned more than once.

CONCLUSIONS

In the event of disarmament the aircraft industry as at present constituted would lose markets amounting to some 70 per cent of production, together with contracts financing 80 per cent of its research and development work. 45 per cent of its employees, some 135,000, of which more than half are concentrated in the north west, south west, eastern and southern regions, would immediately become redundant, and the indirect effects of the loss of so high a proportion of development capital would shortly lead to the redundancy of a still higher percentage. In addition to this a large number of electrical, electronic and general engineering firms producing equipment for the industry would be likely to find an average of 10 per cent of their labour force at least temporarily redundant, and individual firms among these would be considerably more seriously affected.

It was generally agreed among the aircraft firms interviewed that the prospects of replacing defence markets with sales of civil aircraft were negligible. Civil markets themselves would almost inevitably contract in the event of disarmament, especially if government help were not given towards maintaining research and development work. Despite the reorganisation of the industry into large units, it is not believed that sufficient private capital would be forthcoming to bear these costs.

The situation in the aircraft industry in the event of disarmament would in fact depend very largely on the degree of government assistance given, but in view of the length of time involved in aircraft development it is difficult to see how even the most generous financial aid could help companies to survive the first few years. It seems probable that some government contracts would have to be given for existing types of civil aircraft, either for the civil airlines to make what use they could of them, or for gifts or lease to other countries in the form of aid, if large scale unemployment and the almost total running down of production facilities were not to follow. It might also be possible to encourage the growth of a market for small executive aircraft, possibly by tax reliefs to customers, in a relatively short space of time. The government could provide the industry with new markets in the long term by placing development contracts, as so many of the firms interviewed suggested, for supersonic and vertical-take-off civil aircraft, and for new types of aircraft, such as the Hovercraft, for inter-city and cross-channel communications. These forms of expenditure would not affect production lines for several years, and the same would be true of a space research programme. Since, however, designers were said to be the most difficult type of aircraft employee to transfer to other industries, one major problem would at least be solved.

Whatever government action were taken, it seems clear that there would have to be considerable reductions in the capacity of the aircraft industry. This might be achieved without involving large-scale redundancies through assisting individual firms to diversify into other sectors. The aircraft manufacturers interviewed were not on the whole optimistic about the possibilities of diversification, although manufacturers of aircraft equipment, who were already diversified to a large extent, saw this as the principal solution to the problem. Some useful comparisons could perhaps be drawn with the experience of the American industry in recent years. The change in American defence policy from manned aircraft to missiles, together with the completion by the civil airlines of their re-equipment with modern jets, resulted in a considerable contraction in demand throughout the industry. Both aircraft manufacturers and manufacturers of aircraft equipment reacted to this by diversification. A high proportion of diversification has been into military electronics, but one airframe manufacturer has entered the field of long-range communications and architectural aluminium products, an aero-engine manufacturer produces data transmission systems for civil as well as military aircraft, and another has developed pressurising and air-conditioning systems for high-altitude aircraft of both types. Aircraft equipment manufacturers have diversified still further, changing from sub-assemblies for military aircraft to air-conditioning systems for buildings and stainless steel sinks, and from other aircraft components to aluminium boats and lorries.

These trends in the American industry have been going on for some years. In the event of disarmament they could be accelerated in this country by financial assistance for re-tooling and re-training, while a certain proportion of the industry was maintained in a state to produce more highly developed forms of civil aircraft ten or more years ahead. If this were done a high proportion of the £300 million currently contributed to the industry for defence purposes would have to continue to be spent for some years; the costs of developing a medium-range supersonic airliner alone up to the prototype construction stage have been estimated at up to £200 million, although this particular sum is likely to be shared with the French government.

It should be borne in mind, however, that these conclusions only apply to the current state of the aircraft industry, and even if there is no move towards disarmament it seems probable that the aircraft industry will contract over the next few years. To this extent, the problems likely to be faced in the event of disarmament will be reduced with the passage of time, particularly if the firms within the industry continue their efforts to diversify.

Chapter 8

The Electronics Industry

THE SIZE AND STRUCTURE OF THE INDUSTRY

The electronics industry is a relatively new industry with a very rapid rate of growth. Estimates of the total value of its output vary, as the products of the components side of the industry are incorporated in equipment produced by other sectors of the industry, and it is hard to avoid a certain element of double-counting in production statistics. Definitions of what constitutes electronics production also vary; in this case cables and ancillary products and telephone equipment have been excluded. On this basis the value of production in the U.K. in 1961 is believed to have been in the region of £270 million,[1] of which some £70 million was exported. It is generally agreed that the industry's current output is well over ten times the pre-war figure, and the rate of growth in recent years has been estimated to have been in the region of a cumulative 10 per cent per annum. The rate of growth of some individual firms has been considerably faster.

It is estimated that there are about 450 manufacturers of electronic equipment in this country, of which some 400 produce capital goods and over 80 produce consumer goods. There are also more than 1,300 firms producing components and accessories for the equipment manufacturers. Several manufacturers of equipment, however, also produce components, and the position is further complicated by the fact that at least half the total number of companies concerned with electronics are either firms whose electronic production represents only a minor proportion of their output, or are members of a group for which this is true. Increasingly heavy costs of research and development have resulted in a trend against the smaller firm, and mergers and take-overs have in recent

---

[1] This figure includes research and development carried out on behalf of the government, but not that carried out by firms for their own purposes. See note 1, p. 46.

years become a common characteristic of the industry. The total labour force employed in the Ministry of Labour category 'radio and other electronic apparatus' has remained at about 230,000 since 1959, although it has doubled over the last ten years. In May, 1961 it was 226,900, of which 99,800 were women.

A high level of expenditure on research and development has accompanied the industry's rapid rate of growth. The D.S.I.R. investigation of 1958 showed that an amount equivalent to 12 per cent of net output was being spent on research, a higher proportion than that of any other industry except aircraft. The electronics industry then employed over 7 per cent of the total number of qualified scientists and engineers working in industry, and two-thirds of these were engaged in research and development. The total spent on research and development in electronics in 1961, much of which it is difficult to distinguish from research and development in the aircraft industry, is estimated at £35 million.

Three years ago the output of the electronics industry could be divided into two approximately equal parts, consisting of the 'entertainments' sector on the one hand, and the industrial or capital equipment sector on the other. Since then, however, the growth of the capital equipment sector has outstripped that of the entertainments sector, which now constitutes the smaller part of the industry. The value of production of radio and television sets, record-players and tape recorders declined in 1961 to some £90 million; together with components (spares and exports of parts), the total value of production by the entertainments sector was over £100 million. This is a highly competitive sector of the industry; the market is almost entirely a domestic one in which the main growth in numbers of appliances in use has already taken place, and sales must rely increasingly on replacement demand.

Future growth prospects lie mainly with the industrial and commercial sector, which may be expected to increase its proportion of total electronics production. This sector consists of electronic capital goods used by industry (largely industrial computers and control and test equipment), output of which is estimated at £75 million a year, and of radio-communications equipment, output of which together with radar and navigational aids is estimated at some £90 million a year. This sector also includes business computers and data processing systems for office use, and equipment associated with nuclear energy production and with medical research. The main electronics exports are of radio-communications and navigational aid equipment, and there is a very large potential export market for communications equipment. The most rapid growth taking place at the moment, however, both in domestic and export markets, is in industrial control systems, and this is reflected in the current trend for the bigger firms in the entertainments sector to diversify into the industrial field.

THE ELECTRONICS INDUSTRY AND DEFENCE SPENDING

Production for defence has always been important to the electronics industry, and as defence policy has turned increasingly to reliance on guided missiles and radar, so the proportion of defence in total electronics markets has grown. Guided missiles have in fact been the main stimulus and the main source of finance for most important industrial electronic developments. Defence demand has ranged from these and the equipment associated with them to electronic simulators for training purposes, test gear and control systems and radar and radio equipment. Electronic purchases appear in several items from the defence estimates.

Items from the Defence Estimates showing spending on Electronics

£million 1960/61	1961/62	Item
		Air Estimates:
21·0	21·5	Radio and radar
7·4	6·9	Electrical equipment
65·5[2]	48·0[2]	Armament, ammunition and explosives[1]
		Army Estimates :
4·4	5·3	Signal and radio equipment
8·4	8·8	Miscellaneous warlike stores[1]
		Navy Estimates:
15·2	19·9	Electrical stores and equipment
13·9	19·8	Guns, torpedoes, mines, ammunition[1]

[1] Includes guided missiles.
[2] Revised estimate.

One item from the civil estimates may be added to these; this is expenditure by the Home Office on electronic equipment for civil defence, which was estimated at £0·7 million in 1960/61 and £0·9 million in 1961/62.

The total of these items would obviously greatly exceed the total defence expenditure on electronics. A figure for total defence spending on electronics was published in previous years by the Ministry of Supply; in 1959/60, the last financial year for which this figure is available, the total had reached £57 million. It has been estimated that some 20 per cent of this figure referred to purchases of cable and other products not within the present definition of electronics, so that a more accurate estimate of spending on electronics in that year is in the region of £50 million. An estimate of total spending in 1961 has been quoted as between £60 and £65 million; this would indicate an annual rate of growth of over 10 per cent.

If total electronics production in 1961 was in the region of £270 million, defence purchases therefore accounted for at least 22 per cent. Defence purchases are, however, made largely from the industrial and radio communications sector of the industry, and here defence markets consist of over 35 per cent of total production, to which a further small percentage must be added for sales of military electronic equipment abroad.

Employment figures show defence as having a slightly smaller proportionate importance to the electronics industry as a whole. The number of workers employed on defence contracts for radio and other electronic apparatus during May, 1961 was 39,500. This was just over 17 per cent[1] of the total number employed in electronics. Over 15,000 of the total working on defence contracts were employed in London and the south eastern region; the eastern and southern region had the second highest number with 6,600. The rest were distributed in smaller numbers over the country.

The defence contribution to research and development expenditure is still more important than defence markets are to the capital equipment sector of the industry, being estimated at some 57 per cent of the total for 1961. This does not include research into electronics carried out by government research establishments, which is itself not included in the total of £35 million for the industry's research and development expenditure. The £20 million defence contribution to research consists of payments for work carried out by private firms under government research and development contracts, and it is included in the £60–£65 million estimate of total defence spending on electronic products.

It is interesting to compare these estimates of the importance of defence spending to the British electronics industry with similar estimates for the United States. Defence markets are believed to con-

---

[1] Owing to difficulties of definition, however, there is a strong probability that the true percentage is in fact higher.

stitute 60 per cent of total markets[1] for the American electronics industry. The defence contribution to research and development for all electrical equipment and communications for 1959 amounted to 70 per cent of the total; if this could be broken down for the electronics industry proper the percentage would be likely to be even higher.

RESULTS OF THE QUESTIONNAIRES

Questionnaires were returned by 44 companies engaged in the manufacture of electronic products and supplying some proportion of their output of electronics for defence. Nearly all types of electronics were produced by these companies, the main products supplied for defence purposes being aircraft components and equipment, followed by equipment for ships and guided missiles and including testing and control systems. Twenty of the companies concerned were also manufacturers of non-electronic products, and 15 of these supplied non-electronic products for defence purposes. Three companies were in fact manufacturers of aircraft, and two of guided weapons.

The total number of employees covered by these 44 companies at the time of the return of the questionnaire was 252,916; of this total between 20 and 25 per cent were engaged on defence contracts.

Defence was responsible for over 25 per cent of the turnover of exactly half of these companies. Not many companies were involved to a greater extent than 50 per cent of their turnover; these were all medium or large companies, and the four that attributed as much as 75 per cent of turnover to defence each employed over 3,000 people.

TABLE 25 *Electronics Manufacturers; Percentage of Turnover Attributable to Defence Contracts*

Number of returns

Up to 10%	11–25%	26–50%	51–75%	76–100%	Total returns	Companies employing
3	2	3	nil	nil	8	up to 200
1	3	6	3	nil	13	201–1,000
7	6	3	3	4	23	over 1,000
11	11	12	6	4	44	Total all Companies

[1] That is of total sales rather than of total output.

Defence financing of research and development was rather less prominent than might have been expected. Eleven companies received no contribution to research at all, but eight of these employed less than 500 people. Few firms had more than 50 per cent of expenditure on research financed by defence; the four firms which attributed over 75 per cent of turnover to defence also received over 75 per cent of their research expenditure from defence.

TABLE 26 *Electronics Manufacturers; Percentage of Research and Development Expenditure financed by Defence Contracts*

Number of returns

Nil	Up to 10%	11–25%	26–50%	51–75%	76–100%	Total returns	Companies employing
4	3	1	nil	nil	nil	8	up to 200
4	4	nil	4	1	nil	13	201–1,000
3	7	3	2	3	4	22	over 1,000
11	14	4	6	4	4	43[1]	Total all Companies

[1] One company did not answer the question

Official statistics on the regional distribution of defence work in electronics are shown on page 14. Table 27 shows the information on this point obtained from the questionnaires; this coincides to a large extent with the official figures, although the midland region appears to have a higher proportion of defence work than is actually the case.

TABLE 27 *Electronics Manufacturers: Regional Distribution of Factories with Defence Work*

North	E. & W. Ridings	North Midland	East	London & S.E.	South	Companies employing
nil	nil	nil	nil	7	nil	under 200
nil	nil	nil	2	6	nil	201 to 1,000
1	1	2	4	14	4	over 1,000
1	1	2	6	27	4	Total all Companies

South West	Wales	Midland	North West	Scotland	N. Ireland	Companies employing
nil	nil	nil	nil	nil	nil	under 200
nil	nil	3	1	1	nil	201 to 1,000
2	1	5	4	1	1	over 1,000
2	1	8	5	2	1	Total all Companies

The concentration of work in London and the south eastern region is very marked, but it is particularly heavy for small and medium-sized companies.

In replying to the questions relating to the situation that might be expected to arise if disarmament were to take place, 41 companies made some estimate as to whether their resources were transferable to production for civil use. Nearly 70 per cent considered their production resources to be fully transferable, just over 20 per cent that resources were partially transferable, and the remainder that no transfer would be possible.

TABLE 28 *Electronics Manufacturers; How far Production Resources could be transferred to Civil Work*

Number of returns

Entirely	Partially	Not at all	Companies employing
7	1	nil	under 200
7	4	1	201–1,000
14	6	1	over 1,000
28	11	2	Total all Companies

Two large companies and one medium-sized company who said that resources could be partially transferred added that this would only be to a very small extent. Three companies differentiated between production and research resources; two of these were large companies who stated that, while production resources could be completely transferred, research resources could be only partially transferred, and the third, a medium-sized company, thought that production resources could be transferred completely and research resources not at all.

The possibility of the transfer of resources, as it was pointed out in the previous chapter, does not imply that civil markets will be available for the output involved. Electronics manufacturers made this clear in describing the main problems of disarmament; some 20 per cent saw no prospect of avoiding a permanent contraction in output and in the number of their employees, and a further 24 per cent mentioned the problems of excess capacity and increasing commercial work. A similar proportion expected temporary redundancy over a difficult period of adjustment while civil markets were being built up.

TABLE 29 *Electronics Manufacturers; the Main Problems of Disarmament*
Number of times mentioned

By companies employing under 200	By companies employing 201–1,000	By companies employing over 1,000	Total times[1] mentioned	
nil	4	6	10	Temporary redundancy while commercial work is built up
nil	4	5	9	Excess capacity—how to build up commercial work
nil	5	3	8	Permanent redundancy
3	1	2	6	Indirect effects of a general fall in demand
nil	nil	4	4	Finance for adaptation
1	nil	3	4	How to maintain research expenditure
1	1	nil	2	Lower profits
4	2	3	9[2]	None

[1] The number of mentions exceeds the number of companies questioned since some companies gave more than one answer.
[2] Two of these said that there would be no problems if sufficient warning were given. Five other companies also said that sufficient warning would reduce the severity of their problems.

There is some indication that permanent redundancy is more likely in the case of a medium-sized company than a large one. It is interesting to see that expectation of a general recession as the result of disarmament is not common, and also that the problem of obtaining finance for readaptation is only mentioned four times. The question of finance, not necessarily in the form of a direct grant to the manufacturer, appeared in fact to be much more prominent from the follow up interviews, when the question of government spending after disarmament was discussed in more general terms.

RESULTS OF THE INTERVIEWS

Interviews were carried out with nine of the large and three of the medium-sized firms supplying electronic equipment for defence, and also with two trade associations whose members are drawn wholly or partly from the electronics industry.

Transfer of resources. There was some difference of opinion as to the extent to which resources are in fact transferable. Three companies thought that all employees were fully transferable, while others suggested that some classes of skilled labour employed on defence contracts would be difficult to re-employ. The machinist, at the lowest level of skilled labour, can normally be re-trained in a matter of weeks, but the skilled electronics technician was believed by some companies to be inflexible and only transferable to closely related techniques. One company went so far as to suggest that not more than 20 per cent of their most skilled employees, ranging from qualified scientists to technicians, could easily be moved to other work. Another estimated that some 60 per cent of all grades of employees would need expensive retraining before they could be transferred, and this company employed over 1,000 workers on defence contracts. Scientists and engineers working in research teams were normally believed to be transferable, but it was pointed out that teams have particular qualities and values which are lost if they have to be disbanded.

On the equipment side it was agreed that there was a large proportion of general machinery which was fully transferable. A certain amount of highly specialised equipment was not, and much of this was specifically used for the manufacture of military equipment to higher standards than would be likely to be required for civil work. Some machinery would only be transferable to a civil space programme. More expensive re-tooling would obviously be necessary where a firm began to manufacture a new commercial product than where it adapted a military product to civil use, but firms manufacturing a variety of electronic components for specialist requirements tended to re-tool frequently anyway.

The expansion of civil markets. Nearly all the firms interviewed had existing civil markets which they believed could be expanded if defence work came to an end, with a degree of success which would depend chiefly on the general buoyancy of demand at the time, but also in some cases on supporting government action. The domestic markets most frequently mentioned were those for computers, process control and all measuring instruments, communications, particularly for air services and railways, civil aircraft instruments and equipment, and, to some extent, radio and television. Several firms already manufactured goods for commercial markets which were based on a product originally made for defence; this was particularly true of civil aircraft instruments and industrial computers and process control systems. There was no doubt that there are many new civilian applications of electronics to come, and the larger firms in particular mentioned new products for office and industrial automation, communications, space research, medical research and for consumer markets (for example, colour television), to which production capacity could be transferred provided finance were forthcoming.

Some of the companies exported defence products, but these were seldom of major importance as a sales outlet. The most usual civil export markets were in radio and telecommunications equipment, and these were always said to have excellent growth prospects, particularly in the under-developed countries. It was felt by a few manufacturers that the availability of defence contracts had resulted in a relative neglect of export markets, and all agreed that disarmament would act as a considerable stimulus to exports, while at the same time creating a highly competitive situation.

Research and development after disarmament. The withdrawal of government finance for research and development seemed to all the companies interviewed, with only one exception, to be one of the main problems of disarmament, and to five of the companies concerned it appeared the most important problem that would arise. The one exception was a firm in a relatively isolated area, for whom the main problem over research work had always been the shortage of technicians rather than money.

It was generally said that the most important advances in electronics had all been made for defence projects, or had at least been incidental to them. The defence contribution to research in the United States was known to be even higher, and several companies observed that it would be impossible to compete internationally if research expenditure had to be limited to private resources. Even supposing that the governments of other countries ceased to contribute to research, the rate of progress would be drastically slowed down, to the general loss. One company had in fact tried to finance its research and development itself, but had soon been forced to seek government assistance; two others would have preferred to do so, as they resented the necessity of passing on the information acquired to other government contractors, but recognised the impossibility of independence, and one company would have preferred not to have defence contracts at all, but accepted them in order to obtain the facilities for research. Two manufacturers did, however, suggest that industry could increase its own contribution to research, even though it could not finance it entirely.

Previous experience of cuts in defence spending. The companies interviewed were asked if they had had any previous experience of problems arising from cuts in defence spending. Five manufacturers had in fact suffered from cuts or delays in defence contracts, and four others said that they had been careful not to become too heavily involved in defence work for this reason. Two companies had been affected by the change of policy over the Blue Streak rocket; in one case this had led to redundancy for 600 production staff, and the company was left with a surplus factory. As this was in the London area it is believed that the redundant workers did not have much difficulty in finding new jobs; the company subsequently made great efforts towards diversification, entering the fields of automatic weighing machinery and industrial controls. The other company affected had just avoided redundancy by transferring staff to private venture work until fresh government orders came in; this meant a year of bad financial results.

Other examples of cuts in defence contracts were given, some of which had resulted in redundancy. On the whole, however, it seemed that electronics manufacturers had been able to avoid sudden dismissals in these circumstances, and had relied instead on the reduction of their labour force through natural wastage until such time as new defence orders were obtained.

Government action on disarmament. There was little disagreement between electronics manufacturers as to the sort of government action which would be necessary if disarmament were to take place. Nearly all manufacturers believed that large scale redundancy and financial hardship would result if strong measures were not taken, and more than one expressed concern that there was not as far as they knew any overall plan for this eventuality. It was frequently pointed out that disarmament, if it came, would be likely to have very rapid effects on defence markets, although adjustment to purely civil demand would take from one to three years. Government measures would therefore be necessary both to cover the interim period of adaptation and to influence the long term changes in the pattern of the industry.

In the short term, it was suggested by some manufacturers, the main objective should be to keep up employment, and this could mean that unwanted products would continue to be made or that the sale of a firm's commercial products, for which markets could not immediately be expanded, should be guaranteed. A time limit would be necessary for any element of subsidy to production. In the longer run, however, the effect of government measures should be to encourage and assist firms to find new markets. Four firms suggested that financial aid would be necessary for re-tooling, or that special borrowing powers should be provided for badly hit firms. The main new or expanded markets into which it was believed that the industry could move were industrial automation equipment, communications and space research, civil aircraft equipment and consumer durable goods. Two firms felt strongly that industry should be encouraged towards further automation, and that this was in fact already necessary in view of the progress made towards automation in the U.S. Encouragement should take the form either of tax reliefs to automating firms or grants for this purpose, and direct action could be taken in the case of the nationalised industries. Other manufacturers, however, pointed out that, although they themselves hope to expand the market for industrial controls, its rate of expansion is limited by the number of systems engineers available, since every control system has to a certain extent to be individually planned, and that it is not a form of output that employs many production staff.

It was generally believed that large potential markets for radio-communications existed abroad, particularly in the under-developed countries, and some manufacturers suggested that increased aid to these countries would result in the expansion of these markets. One manufacturer thought that aid might take the form of gifts of communications equipment. Similar projects, such as government orders for civil aircraft and the associated equipment for lease to under-developed countries, were mentioned, and a space communications programme, probably carried out in conjunction with other governments, was suggested to replace much of the existing guided missile demand.

It was not always believed that government action should take the form of direct orders for electronic equipment. As in the case of industrial automation markets, manufacturers suggested that measures of general tax relief would stimulate sales. In particular, larger disposable incomes for consumers were expected to expand radio and television markets, and colour television was quoted as a new field for the industry.

Possibly the most important field for government action, however, was thought to be that of research and development. Nearly all manufacturers believed that research and development for civil purposes would have to continue to be financed on almost the same scale as research for defence is now. There was some difference of opinion as to the way in which this should be done; some companies suggested that the government should place civil contracts for research projects concerning space, communications, medicine, and all other important fields in the same way as defence contracts are given to individual firms. Others would prefer wider measures of tax relief to encourage expenditure on research by private firms, or guarantees that losses incurred in research would be made good; two manufacturers believed that industry could finance a larger proportion of research and that tax relief should be given to encourage this, although government contracts would still be necessary. Direct aid to projects carried out by certain firms was also suggested, according to a programme of essential developments drawn up by the D.S.I.R. or N.R.D.C.

It was clear in any case that research expenditure in electronics is one of the most important economic problems likely to be associated with disarmament. One manufacturer remarked that research for defence had so far provided not only the finance for progress in electronics, but also, because of the high standards set and the sense of urgency involved, most of the stimulus. He suggested that government projects for research in the application of electronics to agriculture and medicine might provide the necessary alternative inspiration.

CONCLUSIONS

If disarmament were to take place in the near future, the electronics industry as a whole would be faced with the problem of replacing over £60 million of its total markets (over 20 per cent of total output) in order to find alternative work for something over 17 per cent of its labour force. The main burden would fall on the manufacturers of electronic capital goods, who would have to replace markets for at least 35 per cent of their total output, and one of the most crucial problems would be that of maintaining the present rate of technical advance, since expenditure on research and development would be cut by over one half.

The expansion of existing markets and the creation of new ones to the extent of over 20 per cent of output is not an insoluble problem to an industry which has been accustomed to grow at a rate approaching 10 per cent per annum, and in which individual firms have grown by more than twice that rate. It is nevertheless a problem on a sufficient scale to require a certain degree of government assistance. In existing circumstances, for example, the whole of the alternative £60 million would have to be found in capital goods markets, since the 'entertainments' sector is relatively static and a high degree of market saturation has in fact been reached in the U.K. Sales of radio and television sets are, however, extremely sensitive to changes in purchase tax and in hire purchase restrictions. Although it is unlikely that a government would feel able to give the income tax relief that some of the manufacturers interviewed hoped for in the first few years after disarmament had begun, a relaxation of hire purchase controls and some cuts in purchase tax would be an obvious means of assistance to the electronics industry. Sales of radio and television sets rose in value by 28 per cent between 1958 and 1959 after the lifting of all hire purchase controls in the autumn of 1958. This degree of stimulation would be unlikely to occur a second time, partly because of the more cautious hire purchase practice now current and partly because the market is at a much higher ownership level. Replacement demand, however, could well be influenced to the extent of rising by an additional 10 to 15 per cent, and assuming a home market in the region of £75 million, this could provide some £10 million towards the necessary £60 million. In the long run, colour television, thermo-electric refrigerators and electronic equipment for motor vehicles could lead to a further expansion of consumer markets, but these developments are not near enough to be of use in current circumstances.

The remaining £50 million would have to be provided by markets for capital goods. Current sales of radio-communications, radar and navigational aids amount to some £90 million. This market has a very large growth potential. Considerable advances have recently been made in automatic landing systems and in other types of control for aircraft, and in these and in marine and railway communications sales could increase both to the home market and to other industrialised countries. There would be a strong case for government spending on radar and communications equipment for harbours, airports and the railways as an immediate alternative to defence spending as soon as disarmament began, which might increase sales by 10 per cent or more. There are large potential markets for communications in the developing countries, and the increase in aid to these which should result from disarmament would certainly in the long term stimulate sales; it seems doubtful, however, whether this could be brought about in time to have much effect on the immediate problem.

Another market dependent on government action is that provided by space research. A decision to embark on or to expand the European satellite research programme could follow disarmament; the British contribution to this has been estimated at £15 million to £20 million a year.

The remaining large markets for capital goods are for industrial controls and computers for industry and commerce. The current market for industrial controls is at about £30 million, and it is growing at a rate of 20 per cent per annum. British manufacturers complain that industrialists in this country have been considerably slower to adopt these systems than have their American counterparts, and urge that a system of tax relief should follow disarmament to encourage automation. This seems an unlikely action by any government at a time when there was general concern for the maintenance of full employment, and it is also difficult to imagine a much faster rate of growth in view of the availability of systems engineers and the necessity of individual planning. It might be easier to encourage spending on computers, now amounting to some £9 million a year, and direct purchases for government departments would again be a possibility.

A very rough estimate of how the greater part of the £60–£65 millions missing from electronics markets in the event of disarmament could be replaced might be as follows:—

£million

10   Entertainments sector after lifting of h.p. restrictions, reducing purchase tax

15   Purchases and contributions towards research in communications and control equipment for aircraft, harbours, railways, together with some natural growth in civil communications

10[1] Contribution to European space programme

5   Increased communications exports to under-developed countries

8   Growth (largely unassisted) of sales of industrial control systems

3   Assisted growth of sales of computers

5   Miscellaneous (medical equipment etc.); purchases and research

[1] Estimated electronics content of total contribution.

This implies that there would be little actual growth in total electronics markets for two or three years after disarmament began, but no major setback.

Both in the short and in the longer term, however, the maintenance and expansion of electronics markets would depend upon government assistance to research and development. Export sales of communications equipment, industrial controls and computers depend upon British manufacturers remaining in the forefront of technological progress, and disarmament would mean an intensification of international competition which would probably involve increased rather than diminished expenditure on research. Industry could enlarge its expenditure to some extent, but the size of the individual sums concerned must always necessitate government aid. It is unlikely that the present defence contribution of £20 million to research could be safely reduced at all.

Chapter 9

The Shipbuilding
and Marine Engineering Industries

The value of net output by the shipbuilding, shiprepairing and marine engineering industries was recorded by the 1958 Census of Production as £227 million, of which just over £20 million was attributed to the Royal Dockyards. The value of total sales in the same year was £493 million.

Shipbuilding capacity, apart from new naval construction, has been estimated at 1·6 million gross tons a year, but production has never reached this figure. The tonnage of merchant ships completed has declined in recent years.

Tonnage of Merchant Ships Completed in the U.K.
million gross tons

1958	1·46
1959	1·38
1960	1·30
1961	1·38

In 1958 nine enterprises were responsible for almost half the output of the three industries combined, while the production of the remaining half was spread over a large number of firms. There are in the region of 70 shipyards, of which 27 are capable of building ships of over 20,000 gross tons, and some hundreds of small enterprises engaged in repairing and boat building. There are over 50 marine engineering firms, manufacturing diesel engines, steam turbines, boilers and gearing, and in addition to these 26 shipyards have their own engineering works. Marine engine builders normally supply ships of over 1,000 gross tons; a total of some 35 engine builders supplies an average 160 ships a year of this size. Smaller ships' engines are usually made by 'land' diesel engineering firms.

In May, 1961 the numbers employed in shipbuilding and shiprepairing were 164,300 men and 8,800 women, and in marine engineering 66,500 men and 4,200 women, a total for both industries of 243,800. This was 37,600 lower than in the same month of 1958.

Expenditure on research and development by individual firms was estimated in 1958 at £282,000 for the shipbuilding industry and £1,200,000 for marine engineering. A further £1 million may be added, however, for contributions to co-operative research made by the industries and by the Department of Scientific and Industrial Research and the Admiralty. This would bring total expenditure on research to 1·7 per cent of net output[1] by the shipbuilding (exclusive of ship-repairing) and marine engineering industries; the proportion for marine engineering alone would be higher at 4·4 per cent. Until 1962, when they were merged, each industry maintained a research association which also received contributions from the D.S.I.R. and the Admiralty. In addition the industries pay for some of the work carried out by the D.S.I.R. Expenditure on research by the shipbuilding industry is not large, but it has grown in recent years.

The problems of the British shipbuilding industry are to a large extent similar to those affecting shipbuilding all over the world. World shipbuilding capacity continued to expand between 1950 and 1959, whereas demand began to fall in 1957. World launchings in 1959 totalled 8·7 million gross tons, 2·3 million gross tons less than world capacity, which is now sufficient to replace the whole of the world fleet in ten years. The average life of a ship is twenty years, and the increasing speed and efficiency of modern vessels has resulted in a slowing down of the growth in demand for new tonnage for new seaborne trade to an estimated 3·5 per cent a year. World production is expected to continue to fall sharply until 1964, when it will still be well below world capacity.

The British shipbuilding industry, however, has not only experienced the general problem of falling demand but has also suffered from a decline in its share of world markets. In 1951 the U.K.'s share of world ship exports was 49 per cent; by 1959 this had fallen to 3 per cent. Some part of this decline was the inevitable result of the building up of shipbuilding industries abroad after the war, but it must also be attributed to a lack of competitiveness on the part of the British industry. Various factors account for this; the existence of too many small production units, failure to modernise or to spend sufficiently on research, and restrictive practices on behalf of both management and unions, have all

---

[1] This may be compared with the figure for all manufacturing industries of 3·8 per cent.

been frequently suggested. Efforts have been made in recent years to redress the situation. Modernisation and re-equipment of shipyards has been taking place at an increasing rate since 1956, as a result of which a number of U.K. shipyards are, or will be, fully competitive with the new yards in Japan, West Germany and Sweden. Expenditure on research and development has risen; a trend towards mergers has begun, and the recent decision of the two largest shipbuilding craft unions to unite is another step towards improved efficiency.

In recent months the results of modernisation have begun to show. Nearly 50 per cent of new orders placed with British shipyards during the first quarter of 1962 were for overseas registration, as compared with under 8 per cent for the same period of 1961. New orders by British owners remain low, however, and it is clear that production by the two industries will fall still lower in the near future. The Shipbuilding Advisory Committee has estimated the total demand for merchant ships likely to be available to British shipyards from 1961 to 1965 inclusive as follows:—

Total Demand Available to U.K. Shipyards, 1961–1965

gross million tons

2·5	Non-tanker
1·5	U.K. tankers
0·75	Foreign tankers
4·75	Total

1·38 million tons of this total was completed in 1961. If this estimate proves correct average production in the years 1962 to 1965 will be under 900,000 gross tons a year, over 700,000 tons below capacity, or 35 per cent below production in 1961. It is inevitable that the total numbers employed in the industries will fall by some similar proportion.

THE INDUSTRY AND DEFENCE SPENDING

The greater part of new ships for the Royal Navy are built in private shipyards under contract from the Admiralty. A small proportion are built in the Royal Dockyards, and engines and machinery for these are bought in from outside suppliers. The bulk of contracts for naval engines goes to the marine engineering industry; 'land' turbine makers in heavy electrical industry are often paid royalties by the Admiralty for engines made under their licenses, but do not receive more than a very small proportion of total naval engine expenditure.

The Dockyards are responsible for the greater part of naval repair work, but some repairs, and particularly major conversions, are carried out by private yards.

Defence expenditure on new ships and their engines, alterations and repairs is shown in the Navy Estimates.

Items from the Navy Estimates showing Defence Expenditure on New Ships, alterations and repairs

£million

1960/61	1961/62	
		Contract work:
29·9	27·5	New construction[1]
7·4	7·9	Repairs
37·3	35·4	Total
		Dockyard work:
8·0	6·6	New construction
37·1	41·7	Repairs
82·4	83·7	Total

[1] Vote 8, Section III. One-third of the total figure for new construction has been deducted to allow for the value of general machinery not attributable to shipbuilding or marine engineering output.

Purchases of warships by overseas customers are frequently made through the Admiralty, so that the total of £84 million for 1961/62 includes both home defence expenditure in the shipbuilding industries and the greater part of defence exports. Although total defence spending has changed little since 1960/61, it is nearly 30 per cent higher than in 1957/58.

Total output by the shipbuilding industries in 1961 is not known. It is however estimated to be approximately half way between net output and total sales, and neither of these is believed to have changed significantly since 1958. In order to be able to compare the importance of defence markets to the shipbuilding industries with the importance of defence markets to the aircraft and electronics industries, this estimate of total output, which amounts to £357 million, is used as a basis for the calculations which follow. The shipbuilding industry differs from the industries previously considered in having a large government-owned sector; the estimate of total output excluding output by the Dockyards is £325 million.

Total defence expenditure in the shipbuilding industries in 1960/61 and in 1961/62 amounted to just over 23 per cent of estimated total output in each year. Total defence expenditure in the private sector of the industry alone amounted to just over 11 per cent in 1960/61, and to just under 11 per cent in 1961/62, of estimated total output by the private sector.

These percentages are very similar to the percentages of shipbuilding employees engaged on defence work. In the private industry 9·6 per cent of employees are engaged on defence work, while nearly 11 per cent of output consists of defence work; this reflects the slightly higher value of output per man employed on naval work.

Shipbuilding, Shiprepairing and Marine Engineering; Numbers Employed on Defence Work as at May, 1961

thousands

Total employed in private industry	Number employed on contract defence work	Percentage employed on contract defence work	
137·1[1]	11·3	8·2	Shipbuilding and repairing
70·7	8·6	12·2	Marine engineering
207·8	19·9	9·6	Total

Total employed	Number employed in Dockyards	Percentage of total employed on contract and Dockyard defence work	
173·1	36·0[1]	27·3	Shipbuilding and repairing
70·7	nil	12·2	Marine engineering
243·8	36·0[1]	22·9	Total

[1] Estimate

The Admiralty placed research and development contracts worth nearly £12 million with private firms in 1961/62, but very little of this sum can be attributed to shipbuilding or marine engineering. The marine engineering research association has received Admiralty contributions, and one large shipbuilding firm is associated with the Admiralty in a marine engineering research department, but the total defence contribution to research and development in shipbuilding and marine engineering is unknown.

The system of placing Admiralty contracts for shipbuilding and repairing has been changed in recent months to a method of competitive tendering. This has made it easier for the large firms to gain defence contracts, so that the impact of defence spending upon the industry is likely to become increasingly concentrated upon a few companies. At present, however, a few small firms are still fairly heavily involved in defence work.

RESULTS OF THE QUESTIONNAIRES

Questionnaires were returned by 15 shipbuilding firms, 11 of which were also marine engineers. Nine of these companies built ships under Admiralty contracts, ranging from guided missile destroyers and submarines to frigates, minesweepers and patrol boats, and three companies had also carried out engineering defence work. Four firms only carried out repair or conversion work for defence purposes, and two only supplied equipment. Two firms were also manufacturers of armaments, and one of radar and military bridging equipment.

These 15 companies employed a total of 108,860, of which approximately 17 per cent were said to be employed wholly, or mostly, on defence work.

Questionnaires were also returned by 33 other firms which supplied a wide variety of naval equipment under defence contracts. The majority of these were general or electrical engineers; they included two marine engine builders, two suppliers of auxiliary machinery, and two suppliers of marine boilers. The other products were batteries and other electrical equipment, engine room communications and electronic equipment, and numerous components for electrical and electronic equipment. Eight firms also manufactured equipment for aircraft and six manufactured armaments or components for them.

These 33 companies employed a total of 172,265, of which approximately 25 per cent were said to be employed wholly, or mostly, on defence work.

Just under half of all the shipbuilding firms replying to the questionnaire were not involved in defence contracts to a greater extent than 10 per cent of turnover, and two-thirds of all the firms were not involved by more than 25 per cent. Only two firms, one large and one medium, were involved by more than 50 per cent of their turnover. The majority of the 15 respondents were large firms enploying over 1,000 people.

TABLE 30 *Shipbuilding and Shiprepairing Firms; Percentage of Turnover attributable to Defence Contracts*

Number of returns

Up to 10%	11–25%	26–50%	51–75%	76–100%	Total returns	Companies employing
1	nil	nil	nil	nil	1	up to 200
2	1	nil	1	nil	4	201–1,000
4	2	3	1	nil	10	over 1,000
7	3	3	2	nil	15	Total all Companies

Defence was still less important to shipbuilding companies as a source of finance for research and development. More than half of the respondent firms received no contribution to research from defence contracts, and only one of the two firms that were heavily dependent on defence for their turnover was also dependent on defence for research expenditure.

TABLE 31 *Shipbuilding and Shiprepairing Firms; Percentage of Research and Development financed by Defence*

Number of returns

nil	Up to 10%	11–25%	26–50%	51–75%	76–100%	Total returns	Companies employing
1	nil	nil	nil	nil	nil	1	up to 200
3	nil	nil	nil	1	nil	4	201–1,000
4	5	nil	nil	nil	nil	9	over 1,000[1]
8	5	nil	nil	1	nil	14	Total all Companies

[1] One firm's percentage was not available.

Half of the shipbuilding respondents were situated in Scotland and the north. The two largest companies had shipyards in more than one region.

TABLE 32 *Shipbuilding and Shiprepairing Firms; Regional Distribution of Factories with Defence Work*

North	E. & W. Ridings	North Midland	East	London & S.E.	South	Companies employing
nil	nil	nil	nil	1	nil	up to 200
nil	nil	nil	1	nil	nil	201–1,000
3	1	nil	nil	1	2	over 1,000
3	1	nil	1	2	2	Total all Companies

South West	Wales	Midland	North West	Scotland	N. Ireland—	Companies employing
nil	nil	nil	nil	nil	nil	up to 200
1	1	nil	nil	1	nil	201–1,000
1	nil	nil	2	4	1	over 1,000
2	1	nil	2	5	1	Total all Companies

The last two questions on the questionnaire were concerned with the situation that would arise if disarmament were to take place. The companies were asked how far resources could be transferred to civil work, and what they felt were the main problems which they would be likely to have to face if defence contracts ceased. With one exception all the shipbuilding firms replied that resources were fully transferable. The exception was one large firm which mentioned the redundancy of some special plant. The main problem most often stated was how to find alternative merchant shipbuilding markets in the present state of world demand. More than one firm observed that although resources were theoretically transferable, it was most unlikely that alternative work would be forthcoming.

TABLE 33 *Shipbuilding and Shiprepairing Firms; the Main Problems of Disarmament*

Number of times mentioned

8   How to find new merchant markets

3   Redundancy while finding new markets;
     consequent loss of skilled labour from the district

2   More severe competition

3   None

Just over half of the 33 companies supplying naval equipment were not concerned with defence work to a greater extent than 10 per cent of their turnover, and only five were involved by more than 25 per cent. With one exception, these five were all large companies. They supplied navigational equipment, oxygen equipment for naval aircraft, and electronic equipment for ships and submarines. All five of these companies also supplied equipment for use in aircraft.

TABLE 34 *Firms Supplying Naval Equipment; Percentage of Turnover attributable to Defence Contracts*

Number of returns

Up to 10%	11–25%	26–50%	51–75%	76–100%	Total returns	Companies employing
3	1	nil	nil	1	5	up to 200
5	4	nil	nil	nil	9	201–1,000
9	6	2	1	1	19	over 1,000
17	11	2	1	2	33	Total all Companies

Defence made no contribution to the research expenditure of nearly half of these companies, and for nine more it constituted under 10 per cent of the total. Six companies derived more than 25 per cent of their research expenditure from defence contributions; these were the same five that were dependent on defence to a greater extent than 25 per cent of their turnover, with the addition of a firm involved in the nuclear submarine programme.

TABLE 35 *Firms supplying Naval Equipment; Percentage of Research and Development financed by Defence*

Number of returns

nil	Up to 10%	11–25%	26–50%	51–75%	76–100%	Total returns	Companies employing
4	nil	nil	1	nil	nil	5	up to 200
5	4	nil	nil	nil	nil	9	201–1,000
5	5	3	1	2	2	18	over 1,000[1]
14	9	3	2	2	2	32	Total all Companies

[1] One firm's percentage was not available.

Firms manufacturing naval equipment were generally widely distributed over the country, except for some concentration on London and the south east.

TABLE 36 *Firms supplying Naval Equipment; Regional Distribution of Factories with Defence Work*

North	E. & W. Ridings	North Midland	East	London & S.E.	South	Companies employing
nil	nil	nil	I	4	nil	up to 200
I	nil	I	2	2	nil	201–1,000
nil	2	3	4	8	2	over 1,000
I	2	4	7	14	2	Total all Companies

South West	Wales	Midland	North West	Scotland	N. Ireland	Companies employing
I	nil	nil	nil	nil	nil	up to 200
2	nil	2	nil	I	nil	201–1,000
I	nil	3	6	4	nil	over 1,000
4	nil	5	6	5	nil	Total all Companies

The majority of manufacturers of naval equipment believed that, in the event of disarmament, resources at present engaged in defence work would be fully transferable to civil uses. Eight manufacturers said that resources would only be partially transferable; two of these mentioned research facilities as being largely non-transferable and one anticipated a 15 per cent redundancy in plant. Three firms said that resources would not be transferable at all in ordinary circumstances; these were all large firms supplying equipment for aircraft and armaments as well as ships and were all involved in defence to a greater extent than 26 per cent of turnover.

TABLE 37 *Firms supplying Naval Equipment; How far Production Resources could be Transferred to Civil Work*

Number of returns

Entirely	Partially	Not at all	Companies employing
4	1	nil	up to 200
8	nil	nil	201–1,000
9	7	3	over 1,000
21	8	3	Total all Companies

The main problems mentioned as being likely to arise in the event of disarmament were thought to be the indirect effects of a general decline in industrial activity and in particular in the engineering sector, and of redundancy of part of the labour force if new markets could not be found or until new lines of production could be developed. Seven firms, however, felt that this situation would present no problems at all.

TABLE 38 *Firms Supplying Naval Equipment; Main Problems of Disarmament*

Number of times mentioned

8	Indirect effects of a general fall in demand
9	Redundancy
2	How to replace research expenditure
5	How to find new markets—excess capacity
7	None

RESULTS OF THE INTERVIEWS

Interviews were carried out with one major shipbuilding concern and with six manufacturers of naval equipment, with a view to obtaining more detailed information on the problems of the transfer of resources and on the situation that would be likely to arise in the shipbuilding and marine engineering industries in the event of disarmament.

Labour, plant and equipment were said by most manufacturers to be fully transferable to civil work. The same labour and tooling could be used to build warships or merchant vessels, but the transfer of shipbuilding resources to general engineering production was said to be difficult, particularly without relevant management experience. A problem peculiar to shipbuilding is the unusually high percentage of skilled labour employed; some 60 per cent of the labour force in a large shipyard consists of skilled men who have served five-year apprenticeships, and a further 15 per cent consists of apprentices. This factor makes temporary redundancy while new commercial work is found a major problem, since if skilled men leave the area they are unlikely to be replaceable on a sufficient scale.

Manufacturers of navigational instruments, engine room communications, marine boilers and auxiliary machinery all envisaged no difficulty in transferring either labour or equipment to commercial work of a similar type, and three firms said that resources could also be transferred to new types of commercial output. Difficulties were mentioned over some equipment for specialised lines by one producer of electrical equipment, and a large manufacturer of electronic equipment thought that a high percentage of both plant and labour was non-transferable. The views of this firm have been included in more detail in the section on electronics.

Manufacturers' opinions were obtained on how far existing commercial markets could be expanded and what new markets could be opened up in order to replace defence sales. There was little hope of expanding merchant shipbuilding; it was in fact observed that capacity in the shipbuilding industry would have to be reduced in the near future. A manufacturer of navigational instruments expected existing markets to decline slightly, since the trend is towards bigger ships rather than larger numbers. Export markets for marine engines and boilers and engine room communications were, however, expected to grow.

Some firms had already begun to diversify into new markets; from shipbuilding into general engineering, from electrical and electronic naval equipment into computers and automatic control systems, and from marine into 'land' engineering. The manufacturers of naval equipment all felt that diversification could be further increased; this was more doubtful for the shipbuilding firm.

The general view of the effect of disarmament on the shipbuilding industry was that it would only be the addition of one more problem to an already serious situation. The government help which would be required if disarmament were to take place may be needed in this industry in any case. Suggestions as to the sort of government action that might be taken were those of incentives to shipowners to encourage earlier scrapping, and heavier spending on any sectors of the economy which might give rise to new demand for shipping. The only example quoted here was that of the railways, which could be enabled to enlarge their coastal fleet. Financial assistance for modernisation of shipyards was said to be unnecessary since the most efficient shipbuilding firms would have to find the money for this anyway, and capacity should be reduced to some extent. Provision for research and development was mentioned by two manufacturers of electronic naval equipment, and other firms suggested that low-interest loans should be made available to companies during the transition period.

CONCLUSIONS

It can be estimated that some 23 per cent of total output by the shipbuilding, shiprepairing and marine engineering industries, including the Dockyards, goes to home defence markets. The proportion for the industry exclusive of the Dockyards is in the region of 11 per cent, and the proportion of labour employed in the private industry on defence work is lower still at 9·6 per cent. The contribution made by defence work to research and development expenditure is not known, but since total expenditure by the industry is small it is likely to constitute an appreciable proportion of it.

Defence markets appear on the whole to be most important to a few large firms within the shipbuilding industry, as well as to a few large manufacturers of naval equipment. The main problem of disarmament is clearly how to replace defence markets with civil work. There are very few prospects of this within merchant shipbuilding, where output is on the contrary expected to be reduced over the next few years in any event, although resources are theoretically transferable from defence to civil production. It is not easy to transfer shipbuilding resources to general engineering products, particularly because of the high proportion of skilled labour involved. Marine engineering and naval equipment firms are in a more favourable position from this point of view.

The kind of government action suggested which might be taken to help these industries in the event of disarmament included incentives to shipowners to encourage earlier scrapping, spending on other sectors of the economy which could give rise to shipping demand, and long term low-interest loans for modernisation and for further credit facilities for customers, and for help to companies to diversify where possible into other industries. It seems possible, although no government intentions have so far been announced, that some of these measures may be necessary in any case, to help the industry to make reductions in output without causing severe local unemployment, so that experience in dealing with these problems may well have been gained before that of disarmament could arise. Reductions in output may however tend to make the industry still more dependent on defence markets, since these are the main markets to have grown in recent years, and are among the few markets in which demand can be relied upon to remain steady in the near future.

Chapter 10

Other Industries

MOTOR VEHICLE MANUFACTURING

The Industry and Defence Spending

Net output by the motor vehicle manufacturing industry was shown in the 1958 Census of Production to be just under £403 million. Total sales in the same year amounted to £1,220 million; this figure involves a certain amount of double counting, as it includes sales of parts and accessories within the industry. Sales of passenger cars fell sharply in 1961, after having risen continuously over the previous five years. Total deliveries of passenger cars, commercial vehicles, industrial trucks and tractors amounted to an estimated £861 million in 1961. This total also includes deliveries by motor manufacturers of spare parts and accessories, but not deliveries by firms engaged solely in the manufacture of spares.

The industry is dominated by five large manufacturing groups, which were responsible for 96 per cent of total passenger car production and 86 per cent of commercial vehicle production in 1960. There are only two other manufacturers of passenger cars with more than 1 per cent of the total market, and four manufacturers of commercial vehicles, together with a limited number of small specialist firms. In addition to these there are a few hundred manufacturers of parts and accessories.

The total number employed in motor vehicle manufacturing in May, 1961 was 418,700.

Defence spending on motor vehicles can be estimated from certain items in the Defence Estimates. This total can most usefully be compared with the total of manufacturers' deliveries shown above. This £861 million, however, does not include deliveries of specialised military vehicles, although it does include sales of ordinary cars, lorries and tractors to the Services. The 1958 Census shows the value of sales of armoured cars and troop carriers, together with fire engines and ambulances, as £4·5 million, and the value of sales of tanks and

Items from the Defence Estimates showing spending on Motor Vehicles
£million

1960/61	1961/62	
4·9	4·4	Air Estimates: Mechanical transport vehicles, also caravans, trailers, spares, accessories, tyres, and repair and conversion by contract.
0·9	1·0	Navy Estimates: Motor transport: purchase, repair and maintenance of vehicles.
22·5	19·0	Army Estimates: Mechanical transport vehicles, purchase and repair of fighting, load-carrying and earth-moving vehicles and their spares.
28·3	24·4	Total

armoured bull dozers as £14 million. This latter total is attributed to the ordnance industry, although in fact a proportion of tanks is made by motor manufacturing firms. It is not possible to discover how much of the total of £18·5 million should be attributed to the motor industry; in the absence of better estimates an arbitrary figure of £10 million has been added to the total of manufacturers' deliveries of ordinary motor vehicles to cover deliveries by the motor industry of specialised military vehicles, giving a final figure of £871 million.

The proportion of defence spending in this total is in the region of 3 per cent. This figure should be reduced slightly by subtracting the proportion of sales of armoured vehicles not attributable to the motor industry, but this would probably be more than balanced by adding the value of exports of military vehicles.

The importance of defence spending to the motor industry appears even smaller from the employment statistics. A total of 8,000 employees in motor vehicle manufacturing were employed on defence work in Great Britain in May, 1961; this was just under 2 per cent of the total labour force.

RESULTS OF THE QUESTIONNAIRES AND INTERVIEWS

Questionnaires were returned by 20 companies manufacturing motor vehicles or components, including tyres and batteries, and supplying them for defence purposes. Eleven of these companies also supplied equipment for use in other defence fields, mainly aircraft equipment or components for weapons manufacture, so that more than half of the questionnaires returned by the motor vehicle industry tend to inflate the importance of defence spending to the industry. The total employed by these 20 companies was 174,566, of which just over 13 per cent were said to be engaged on defence work.

Few companies were involved in defence work to a greater extent than 10 per cent of turnover, and six companies felt that the 'up to 10 per cent' category was misleading and specified that their defence work consisted of less than 3 per cent of turnover.

TABLE 39 *Manufacturers of Motor Vehicles and Components; Percentage of Turnover attributable to Defence Contracts*

Number of returns

Up to 10%	11–25%	26–50%	51–75%	76–100%	Total of returns	Companies employing
nil	nil	1	nil	nil	1	up to 200
5	2	nil	nil	nil	7	201–1,000
9	1	1	nil	1	12	over 1,000
14	3	2	nil	1	20	Total all Companies

Defence spending was of still less importance to research and development work, twelve companies replying that they received no contribution to this expenditure from defence, and five that the contribution was less than 10 per cent of the total.

Branches of the companies where defence work was carried out were concentrated in the midland region.

The majority of these companies felt that the resources now used for defence work could be entirely transferred to civil use. Four of those saying that resources could be only partially transferred added that only a very small proportion would be made redundant.

TABLE 40 *Manufacturers of Motor Vehicles and Components; Regional Distribution of Factories with Defence Work*

North	E. & W. Ridings	North Midland	East	London & S. E.	South	Companies employing
nil	nil	nil	nil	I	nil	up to 200
nil	I	nil	I	I	I	201–1,000
I	I	I	2	2	nil	over 1,000
I	2	I	3	4	I	Total all Companies

South West	Wales	Midland	North West	Scotland	N. Ireland	Companies employing
nil	nil	I	nil	nil	nil	up to 200
nil	nil	3	nil	nil	nil	201–1,000
nil	I	5	4	2	nil	over 1,000
nil	I	9	4	2	nil	Total all Companies

TABLE 41 *Manufacturers of Motor Vehicles and Components; how far Production Resources could be transferred to Civil Work*

Entirely	Partially	Not at all	Total returns	Companies employing
nil	I	nil	I	up to 200
6	nil	nil	6	201–1,000
8	4	nil	12	over 1,000
14	5	nil	19	Total all Companies

Nine companies said that disarmament would present them with no problems, although one made this conditional on a period of warning of at least six months. There was some concern over how to find alternative work.

No interviews were carried out with large companies manufacturing motor vehicles, other than with two companies whose defence work was mainly in other fields and whose views have been reported elsewhere. One large manufacturer of components interviewed expected disarmament to cause few problems except to one small specialised subsidiary

TABLE 42 *Manufacturers of Motor Vehicles and Components; the Main Problems of Disarmament*

Number of times mentioned

By Companies employing up to 200	By Companies employing 201–1,000	By Companies employing over 1,000	Total times mentioned	
1	nil	3	4	Redundancy
1	2	3	6	How to find alternative work
nil	nil	2	2	Indirect effects of a general fall in demand
nil	1	nil	1	Cut in profits
nil	nil	1	1	Increased competition
nil	4	5	9	None

company. In the experience of this group, defence work had been useful to fall back on at times of declining demand, although it was not profitable; it would only be missed for this purpose. Continued government expenditure was thought to be desirable to maintain the general level of demand. Another engineering group had one small subsidiary manufacturing fighting vehicles, and said that the loss of defence work by this company would involve redundancy unless government aid were made available until new markets were found. The loss of contributions to development expenditure would also result in a general slowing down of development work.

CONCLUSIONS

Domestic defence markets do not constitute more than 3 per cent of the main markets of the motor industry. The direct effects of disarmament on the industry as a whole would be very small, although a few specialist manufacturers of commercial vehicles and a few manufacturers of components would suffer appreciable cuts in turnover.

Conditions in the motor vehicle industry (and also in the motor cycle industry, which has been left out of these estimates) change very quickly in response to changes in consumer demand, so that the industry would benefit from the increase in consumer disposable income which could follow disarmament if taxes were reduced. Specialist commercial vehicle companies would be less able to profit from this, and in a few cases there might be small scale redundancies.

MECHANICAL ENGINEERING

THE INDUSTRY AND DEFENCE SPENDING

Figures available from the Defence Estimates are insufficiently broken down to give a useful estimate of defence purchases from the mechanical engineering industry, and in any case the indirect effects of defence spending are likely to be of considerably greater importance to this industry than are direct purchases. Some measure of the importance of defence work to the industry can, however, be obtained from the employment statistics.

Mechanical engineering output, exclusive of the output of vehicles, aircraft or ships or their engines, is covered by thirteen categories in the Standard Industrial Classification. The total employed in these categories, together with the percentage in each employed on defence work, where this is known, is shown in the table below. One category, that of ordnance and small arms, has been omitted, as it will be included in a later section.

Mechanical Engineering; Employment on Defence Work May, 1961

Total employed	Number employed on defence work	Percentage employed on defence work	Standard Industrial Classification
thousands	thousands	per cent	
93·1	3·3	3·5	Metal working machine tools
54·0	2·1	3·9	Engineers' small tools and gauges
39·7	3·0	7·5	Industrial engines
346·4	5·3	1·5	Other machinery[1]
204·5	10·4	5·1	Other mechanical engineering not elsewhere specified
132·6	7·5	5·7	Scientific, surgical and photographic instruments[1]
394·5	n.a.	n.a.	Six other categories
1,264·8	31·6	2·5	Total, twelve categories

[1] Includes some electrical equipment

Only two of the six categories omitted (mechanical handling equipment and office machinery) are likely to include any direct sales for defence purposes, so that total employment on defence work in mechanical engineering, exclusive of ordnance production, can be estimated at some 3 per cent.

RESULTS OF THE QUESTIONNAIRES AND INTERVIEWS

Questionnaires were returned by 32 firms engaged in mechanical engineering and supplying products for defence purposes. Seven of these firms also did electrical or electronic work. Products included ball bearings, machine tools, and general machinery and components for aircraft and aerodromes, ships and armaments. The firms employed a total of 121,511 of which some 5·5 per cent were wholly, or mostly, engaged on defence work.

Only a third of these companies were involved in defence work to a greater extent than 10 per cent of turnover, and the majority of these were small or medium-sized companies.

TABLE 43 *Mechanical Engineering Companies; Percentage of Turnover attributable to Defence Contracts*

Number of returns

Up to 10%	11–25%	26–50%	51–75%	76–100%	Total returns	Companies employing
4	nil	2	nil	nil	6	up to 200
2	2	1	3	nil	8	201–1,000
15	2	1	nil	nil	18	over 1,000
21	4	4	3	nil	32	Total all Companies

The most heavily involved companies were manufacturers of precision ball bearings and aircraft components and ground equipment.

Defence spending was less important to mechanical engineering firms as a proportion of research and development work. Only 5 firms received more than 10 per cent of expenditure from defence contracts. The main concentrations of defence work on mechanical engineering products appear from these returns to be in the London and South eastern and midland regions.

Only 5 mechanical engineering firms, including 2 large ones, said that production facilities would be only partially transferable from defence

TABLE 44 *Mechanical Engineering Companies; Percentage of Research and Development financed by Defence Contracts*

Number of returns

Nil	Up to 10%	11–25%	26–50%	51–75%	76–100%	Total returns	Companies employing
3	2	nil	nil	1	nil	6	up to 200
4	3	nil	nil	1	nil	8	201–1,000
11	4	1	1	1	nil	18	over 1,000
18	9	1	1	3	nil	32	Total all Companies

TABLE 45 *Mechanical Engineering Companies; Regional Distribution of Factories with Defence Work*

North	E. & W. Ridings	North Midland	East	London & S. E.	South	Companies employing
nil	nil	1	nil	3	1	up to 200
nil	1	nil	nil	4	1	201–1,000
2	1	1	3	4	nil	over 1,000
2	2	2	3	11	2	Total all Companies

South West	Wales	Midland	North West	Scotland	N. Ireland	Companies employing
nil	nil	2	nil	nil	nil	up to 200
1	1	nil	nil	nil	nil	201–1,000
2	2	4	1	2	nil	over 1,000
3	3	6	1	2	nil	Total all Companies

to civil work. Few firms expected redundancy to occur if disarmament took place, and the most frequently mentioned problem of disarmament was the indirect effects of a general fall in demand.

Interviews were carried out with six mechanical engineering companies. All of these supplied aircraft, naval or vehicle equipment for defence purposes, and their views have been dealt with more fully in other sections. With the exception of one firm, which was only temporarily involved in defence work to a large extent, they all felt that

TABLE 46 *Mechanical Engineering Companies; the Main Problems of Disarmament*

Number of times mentioned

By Companies employing up to 200	By Companies employing 201–1,000	By Companies employing over 1,000	Total times mentioned	
nil	1	3	4	Redundancy
1	4	6	11	How to find alternative work
2	3	5	10	Indirect effects of a general fall in demand
nil	nil	1	1	Increased competition
1	nil	7	8	None

disarmament would lead to some redundancy unless a long period of warning were given or government assistance towards re-adjustment were provided. Equipment and personnel were said to be largely transferable to civil work.

CONCLUSIONS

Direct defence spending in the mechanical engineering industry is unlikely to affect more than 3 per cent of the total labour force. The indirect effects of any fall in demand for engineering products, and also for ships and aircraft, which might follow disarmament, would probably be much larger, and this was realised by several of the firms replying to the questionnaire. Certain individual companies would in any case suffer from appreciable cuts in turnover.

ELECTRICAL ENGINEERING

THE INDUSTRY AND DEFENCE SPENDING

Manufacturers' deliveries of the principal electrical engineering products in 1960 amounted to just over £659 million for generators and motors (exclusive of machinery immediately incorporated in other production), switchgear, batteries, equipment for vehicles and aircraft, and other industrial items, and to nearly £197 million for domestic electrical appliances and refrigerating machinery. These figures exclude, as far as possible, electronics output.

Spending on electrical equipment by the services is only shown separately in the Air Estimates, where it appears as £7·4 million in 1960/61, falling to £6·9 million in 1961/62. Neither the Navy nor the

Army Estimates distinguish between electrical and electronic equipment. As in the case of mechanical engineering, therefore, the importance of defence spending to the industry can best be indicated by the employment figures.

The following table shows employment in four of the categories of electrical engineering products listed in the Standard Industrial Classification. The categories covering domestic electrical appliances are affected by defence spending to a negligible extent and have been omitted. A further 66,200, together with an unknown figure for refrigerating machinery, were employed in these categories in May, 1961. The category covering electronic equipment has been omitted here and included in a previous section.

Electrical Engineering; Employment on Defence Work May, 1961

Total employed	Number employed on defence work	Percentage employed on defence work	Standard Industrial Classification
thousands	thousands	per cent	
224·2	7·5	3·3	Electrical machinery (generators, motors, switchgear etc.)
62·2	2·4	3·8	Insulated wires and cables
66·6	4·7	7·0	Telegraph and telephone apparatus
144·7	7·4	5·1	Other electrical goods (including equipment for vehicles and aircraft)
497·7	22·0	4·4	Total

The importance of defence spending to the industrial side of the electrical engineering industry can therefore be estimated at 4·5 per cent as far as employment is concerned, although in the case of the heavy electrical engineering sector, and also for the industry as a whole, it is little more than 3 per cent.

THE RESULTS OF THE QUESTIONNAIRES AND INTERVIEWS

Questionnaires were returned by 30 electrical engineering firms supplying products for defence purposes. Five of these firms were also electronics manufacturers. A wide range of products was covered, including generating sets, batteries, switchgear, cables, wire and other equipment, which was supplied to all three services, but most frequently to the Admiralty. The companies employed a total of 108,729 of which just under 4 per cent were engaged on defence work.

Under one-third of all firms were involved in defence work to a greater extent than 10 per cent of turnover, and no firm was involved by more than 50 per cent.

TABLE 47 *Electrical Engineering Companies; Percentage of Turnover attributable to Defence Contracts*

Number of returns

Up to 10%	11–25%	26–50%	51–75%	76–100%	Total returns	Companies employing
2	nil	nil	nil	nil	2	up to 200
7	3	3	nil	nil	13	201–1,000
12	3	nil	nil	nil	15	over 1,000
21	6	3	nil	nil	30	Total all Companies

Defence contracts did not appear to be an important factor in research and development expenditure. Only two firms received a contribution from defence of more than 10 per cent of total expenditure, and no firm received more than 25 per cent.

TABLE 48 *Electrical Engineering Companies; Percentage of Research and Development financed by Defence Contracts*

Number of returns

Nil	Up to 10%	11–25%	26–50%	51–75%	76–100%	Total returns	Companies employing
2	nil	nil	nil	nil	nil	2	up to 200
8	5	nil	nil	nil	nil	13	201–1,000
4	9	2	nil	nil	nil	15	over 1,000
14	14	2	nil	nil	nil	30	Total all Companies

The greatest concentration of electrical engineering firms with defence work was in the London and south eastern region.

The majority of firms felt that in the event of disarmament resources would be fully transferable to civil work. Two of those replying that resources would be only partially transferable specified that plant and materials would be more difficult to transfer than labour.

TABLE 49 *Electrical Engineering Companies; Regional Distribution of Factories with Defence Work*

North	E. & W. Ridings	North Midland	East	London & S. E.	South	Companies employing
nil	nil	nil	nil	2	I	up to 200
I	I	I	nil	6	nil	201–1,000
I	I	nil	4	5	nil	over 1,000
2	2	I	4	13	I	Total all Companies

South West	Wales	Midland	North West	Scotland	N. Ireland	Companies employing
nil	nil	nil	nil	nil	nil	up to 200
I	nil	2	2	nil	nil	201–1,000
nil	nil	4	4	I	nil	over 1,000
I	nil	6	6	I	nil	Total all Companies

TABLE 50 *Electrical Engineering Companies; how far Production Resources could be transferred to Civil Use*

Number of Returns

Entirely	Partially	Not at all	Total returns	Companies employing
2	nil	nil	2	up to 200
11	nil	I	12	201–1,000
11	3	nil	14	over 1,000
24	3	I	28	Total all Companies

Just over one-third of electrical engineering firms did not expect any major problems to arise in the event of disarmament. The problem most frequently mentioned by the remainder was that of the indirect effects of disarmament on the general level of demand.

Interviews were carried out with five electrical engineering companies. As all of these supplied defence products for aircraft, ships or vehicles their views have been given fully in other sections. It was generally agreed that an appreciable period of warning was desirable

TABLE 51 *Electrical Engineering Companies; the Main Problems of Disarmament*

Number of times mentioned

By Companies employing under 200	By Companies employing 201–1,000	By Companies employing over 1,000	Total times mentioned	
nil	3	2	5	Redundancy
nil	3	2	5	How to find alternative work
nil	4	5	9	Indirect effects of a general fall in demand
nil	1	nil	1	Finance for re-adaptation
nil	nil	1	1	Finance for research
2	5	4	11	None

before defence contracts were withdrawn, but there was no strong feeling that government financial assistance would be necessary.

CONCLUSIONS

Defence spending provides just over 4 per cent of employment in the industrial sector of the electrical engineering industry. The proportion is appreciably lower if the consumer sector of the industry is included.

The industry would not face any major problems if disarmament were to take place, and the firms replying to the questionnaire were most concerned about the indirect effects of a general fall in demand. Some specialist manufacturers would suffer significant reductions in turnover, but they appear to be very few in number.

ORDNANCE AND SMALL ARMS, EXPLOSIVES AND FIREWORKS

THE INDUSTRIES AND DEFENCE SPENDING

Net output by the ordnance and small arms industry was shown in the 1958 Census of Production as £36·6 million. Total employment in the industry has declined since then by over 40 per cent, so that production in 1961 may be assumed to have been appreciably lower. Nearly the whole of production is for defence purposes, with the exception of a

Items from the Defence Estimates Showing Spending on Ordnance,
Small Arms, Explosives and Fireworks

£million

1960/61	1961/62	
		Air Estimates:
12·6	7·0	Armaments (bomb, rocket and torpedo gear, ancillary equipment for guided missiles, ground defence weapons and small arms).
59·5	45·6	Ammunition and explosives (also includes bombs, guided missiles, pyrotechnics and torpedoes).
		Navy Estimates:
2·5	1·8	Guns, torpedoes and mines.
11·4	17·9	Ammunition (including bombs, explosives, guided missiles).
		Army Estimates:
10·9	8·3	Guns and small arms.
8·4	8·8	Miscellaneous warlike stores (including guided weapons).
11·0	11·9	Ammunition and explosives
116·3	101·3	Total

Ordnance, Small Arms, Explosives and Fireworks
Employment on Defence Work May, 1961

Total employed	No. employed on defence work	Percentage employed on defence work	Standard Industrial Classification
thousands	thousands	per cent	
30·5	23·3	76·4	Ordnance and small arms
31·2	10·8	34·6	Explosives and fireworks

small proportion of sporting weapons. The greater part of military production is by the Royal Ordnance Factories, and the range of defence products includes all types of guns, together with torpedoes, shell and bomb cases and components, and tanks and other armoured fighting vehicles. It does not include armoured cars, which are classified under the motor industry, nor nuclear weapons, which are produced by other government establishments and by the aircraft and electronics industries.

Net output of explosives and fireworks was shown in the 1958 Census as £30·9 million. This category also includes the manufacture of detonators and fuses, signal rockets, small arms ammunition and the filling of bombs, cartridges and shells. A large proportion of production is for defence purposes, and the greater part of this is also manufactured by government establishments.

Imports and exports of these products cannot be distinguished for the two industries. Under the heading of 'arms, ammunition, military stores and other appliances', imports in 1961 amounted to £5·6 million and exports to £28·7 million. Imports of explosives were very small, and exports amounted to £9·7 million. Items from the Defence Estimates, similarly, cannot be broken down sufficiently to show purchases of ordnance and explosives separately. They also include expenditure on nuclear weapons.

It is not possible from these figures to estimate the proportion of production of ordnance and explosives attributable to defence markets, although it is clear that this is very high. Estimates of the importance of defence spending to the two industries can, however, be obtained from the employment figures.

The percentage for the ordnance and small arms industry would be considerably higher if the numbers working on defence products for export were included, and this would probably also increase the percentage for the explosives and fireworks industry.

RESULTS OF THE QUESTIONNAIRES AND INTERVIEWS

Questionnaires were received from 17[1] companies manufacturing ordnance and small arms or components for these, and supplying them for defence purposes. The majority of these companies were general or electrical engineers, and nearly all of them supplied defence equipment in other fields. Products included guns, components for guns and tanks, and torpedo and gunfire batteries. No questionnaires were returned by companies manufacturing explosives for defence purposes, and ordnance factories as government establishments are dealt with elsewhere.

The total number employed by these companies was 97,484 of which just over 7 per cent were employed on defence work. This reflects the

---

[1] It is possible that one or two of these companies may in fact be manufacturers of components for guided weapons, and should therefore have been classified in the aircraft sector.

large number of component manufacturers included among the 17 companies. Nearly half of the respondent firms were in fact involved in defence work to a greater extent than 10 per cent of turnover, as the following table shows.

TABLE 52 *Manufacturers of Ordnance, Small Arms and Components; Percentage of Turnover attributable to Defence Contracts*

Number of returns

Up to 10%	11–25%	26–50%	51–75%	76–100%	Total returns	Companies employing
3	nil	nil	nil	nil	3	up to 200
3	2	1	1	nil	7	201–1,000
3	2	nil	1	1	7	over 1,000
9	4	1	2	1	17	Total all Companies

TABLE 53 *Manufacturers of Ordnance, Small Arms and Components; Regional Distribution of Factories with Defence Work*

North	E. & W. Ridings	North Midland	East	London & S. E.	South	Companies employing
nil	nil	nil	nil	2	1	up to 200
nil	nil	1	nil	4	nil	201–1,000
nil	nil	nil	nil	1	1	over 1,000
nil	nil	1	nil	7	2	Total all Companies

South West	Wales	Midland	North West	Scotland	N. Ireland	Companies employing
nil	nil	1	nil	nil	nil	up to 200
nil	nil	2	nil	nil	nil	201–1,000
nil	1	4	2	2	1	over 1,000
nil	1	7	2	2	1	Total all Companies

Defence spending was not important to these firms as a percentage of research and development expenditure. Only two companies received more than 10 per cent of research and development expenditure from defence, and both of these carried out their main defence work in other fields.

Defence work by these companies was most highly concentrated in the London and south eastern and in the midland region. The official employment figures, which include the Royal Ordnance Factories, show the greatest concentration in London, followed by the north west.

More than half of these companies believed that the resources now engaged on defence work could be entirely transferred to production for civil purposes. Three firms said that resources could not be transferred at all; two of these were manufacturers of guns.

TABLE 54 *Manufacturers of Ordnance, Small Arms and Components; how far Production Resources could be transferred to Civil Use*

Entirely	Partially	Not at all	Total returns	Companies employing
3	nil	nil	3	up to 200
5	1	1	7	201–1,000
2	3	2	7	over 1,000
10	4	3	17	Total all Companies

The main problems expected to arise from disarmament were those of redundancy and how to obtain alternative work. Four firms did not anticipate any problems.

TABLE 55 *Manufacturers of Ordnance, Small Arms and Components; the Main Problems of Disarmament*

Number of times mentioned

By Companies employing up to 200	By Companies employing 201–1,000	By Companies employing over 1,000	Total times mentioned	
nil	1	3	4	Redundancy
nil	2	2	4	How to find alternative work
1	nil	nil	1	Indirect effects of a general fall in demand
nil	1	nil	1	Finance for re-adaptation
1	1	nil	2	Temporary fall in turnover
nil	1	nil	1	Cuts in profits
1	1	2	4	None

Interviews were carried out with two manufacturers of guns and one of components. One gun manufacturing firm produced weapons for export only, and was accustomed to sporadic sales. A small number of skilled gunmakers was permanently maintained, these being given relatively unskilled work on the company's civil product (a consumer durable good), when gun production was not in process; unskilled women were taken on or laid off as needed to constitute the rest of the gun labour force. The skilled workers were not theoretically transferable to other skilled work, and although alternative work was now found for them when necessary, they were paid for it at an uneconomic rate which would not be justified if they were not being retained for a special purpose. It was estimated that about 50 per cent of machinery could be converted to other engineering purposes; the buildings concerned would be transferable to a heavy engineering product but not to existing consumer durable good production. The impact of international disarmament on this firm would vary with conditions in the market for consumer durable goods; if turnover could be increased on this side, any problems would be considerably reduced.

Another gun manufacturer was shortly to complete a large defence contract, after which the labour involved would become redundant. The company had decided to accept no more defence work, in view of this recurrent problem. Special purpose plant was also going to become redundant, and although the greater part of the labour force was theoretically transferable within the engineering industry, no alternative work was in fact available for them. The company was a member of a group manufacturing other products on which it would now concentrate. This company could not suggest what government action could be taken in the event of disarmament, except for general measures, such as building roads and hospitals, to maintain the general level of demand. The engineering industry was not in a state of growth, and it was difficult to think of any engineering product for which a market could be stimulated by government spending.

CONCLUSIONS

Defence spending accounts for over 75 per cent of employment in the ordnance and small arms industry and for nearly 35 per cent of employment in the explosives and fireworks industry. The dependence on defence work of the ordnance industry, in particular, would appear much greater if employment on military exports were included. The majority of defence workers in both industries are employed in government establishments.

In the event of disarmament almost total redundancy could be expected in the ordnance and small arms industry, with the exception of a small number of workers employed in the manufacture of sporting guns, or of weapons for an international police force. Redundancy would therefore involve something under 30,000 employees. Severe cuts could also be expected in the explosives industry, involving another possible 10,000. In most cases the government would bear direct responsibility for these employees. The provision of work for the skilled workers among them would present severe problems, as there is no obvious related work in the engineering field, but there could be administrative convenience in turning complete government factories over to civil work.

FURTHER INDUSTRIES

Questionnaires were also received from a number of companies in industries supplying such products as clothing, fuel and office equipment to the three Services. There were only two cases in which defence work provided more than 10 per cent of turnover; of these one was a firm manufacturing naval clothing, and the other was a firm providing air conditioning for defence establishments.

Purchases of clothing, food, fuel and other non-specialised equipment by the services would be likely to be maintained to a large extent by ex-Service personnel in the event of disarmament. Service construction of residential accommodation, and a proportion of workshops and other technical buildings, would almost certainly be more than replaced by a civilian building programme which would be an obvious means of employing resources if disarmament were to take place. In any case defence expenditure only constitutes a very small percentage of sales in any of the industries concerned.

Individual firms within these industries which happen to have defence contracts constituting an appreciable proportion of turnover would suffer some temporary inconvenience in the event of disarmament, but within such non-specialised fields as clothing, fuel, or food they would be unlikely to encounter much difficulty in finding alternative markets. The disposal of surplus stocks of uniform and textiles and similar semi-specialised equipment would present a minor problem, but the advent of disarmament would on the whole make extremely little direct impact on any industry other than those which have been dealt with in previous sections.

TABLE 56 *Defence Spending on Clothing, Food and Construction*

£ mn.	Total value of consumers' expenditure(1961)	£ mn.	Defence spending on[1]	Defence as a percentage of total spending
4,989	Food	62·5	Food	1·3
1,687	Clothing	11·4	Clothing	0·7
2,851	Total value of constructional work (1961)	35·6	New works at home	1·2

[1] From the Service Estimates for 1960/61.

The importance of defence spending to the industries considered in this and previous chapters is summarised in the table below:-

TABLE 57 *The Importance of Defence Spending to Certain Industries*

Production		Employment		Research		
Total Value 1961	Defence Spending as a Percent of Production	Total May 1961	Percent on Defence	Total Expenditure 1961	Percent Paid by Defence	Industry
£million	thousands			£million		
435	65–70	298·1	45	125	80	Aircraft
270	22	226·9	17[3]	35	57	Electronics
357[1]	23	243·8	23	2·5	n.a.	Shipbuilding, marine engineering
871[2]	3	418·7	2	n.a.	n.a.	Motor vehicles
n.a.	n.a.	1,264·8	3	n.a.	n.a.	Mechanical engineering
659	n.a.	497·7	4·4	n.a.	n.a.	Electrical engineering (industrial)
36·6[4]	n.a.	30·5	76·4	n.a.	n.a.	Ordnance, small arms
30·9[4]	n.a.	31·2	34·6	n.a.	n.a.	Explosives
2,851	1·2	1,590·0	n.a.	n.a.	n.a.	Construction

Consumers' Expenditure

4,989	1·3	603·2	n.a.	n.a.	n.a.	Food
1,687	0·7	573·0	n.a.	n.a.	n.a.	Clothing

[1] Including the Dockyards.
[2] Manufacturers' deliveries.
[3] Probably higher.
[4] 1958 figures.

PART TWO

THE TRANSFER OF RESOURCES
FROM DEFENCE EXPENDITURE

Chapter 11

Past Experience of Disarmament

The aim of this Part of the survey is to assess the economic consequences of the methods likely to be adopted of using the resources freed in the event of disarmament. A brief look is taken in this chapter at the British and American experience of disarmament after the 1939–1945 war, to see how far, if at all, it is relevant to present day conditions. A more detailed study is made in the next chapter of the measures likely to be needed in the immediate transition period following upon the conclusion of a disarmament treaty, based on the results of Part I of this survey. In the final chapters, four main methods of using the resources released are considered in order that their impact on the economy as a whole, and also on those sectors which currently depend on defence spending, can be determined.

When considering past British experience of disarmament it is perhaps helpful to look at defence expenditure over a number of years to see whether, in fact, it has been an important factor in the economy.

TABLE 58 *Expenditure on Defence*

(Selected Years)

	As percentage of total central current expenditure	As percentage of net national income
1880	33	2·5
1890	38	2·4
1895	39	2·6
1905	41	3·3
1913	38	3·7
1923	14	2·7
1933	14	2·8
1938	22	5·3
1948	22	7·5
1950	25	6·9

The preceding table, taken from 'British Public Finances, 1880–1952'[1] by Ursula K. Hicks, shows quite clearly that, in peacetime, expenditure on defence in the United Kingdom was not of great significance until after the end of the 1939–1945 war.

Moreover, it is pointed out in the book that although rapid advances in defence expenditure in wartime have been responsible for an expansion of the public sector as a whole, defence expenditure itself does not appear to be a permanent cause of expansion, and it has been tending to decline in importance as a proportion of total government current expenditure in this century.

This trend was reversed in the post war years with the increase in defence expenditure for the Korean War, but has since been resumed. Even the sharp rise in defence spending in 1961, for example, did not result in an increase in its share of total government current expenditure.

TABLE 59 *Defence Expenditure and Total Central Government Current Expenditure*

	Defence expenditure [£ million]	Total central government current expenditure [£ million]	Defence expenditure as a percentage of total government expenditure
1950	820	3,697	22·2
1951	1,090	4,067	26·8
1952	1,450	4,626	31·3
1953	1,540	4,839	31·8
1954	1,548	4,940	31·3
1955	1,522	5,102	29·8
1956	1,621	5,418	29·9
1957	1,550	5,555	27·9
1958	1,529	5,934	25·8
1959	1,540	6,238	24·7
1960	1,590	6,664	23·9
1961	1,735	7,307	23·7

Source: National Income and Expenditure Blue Book, 1961 and Preliminary Estimates 1956 to 1961.

Full National Income accounts are not available for the 1939–1945 war years, but a summary of the main statistics was published in a White

[1] Home University Library, Oxford University Press.

Paper entitled 'National Income and Expenditure of the United Kingdom 1938 to 1946', Cmd. 7099. It shows that whereas in 1938 personal expenditure on consumers' goods and services accounted for 80·4 per cent of net national expenditure, and government current expenditure accounted for 14·9 per cent, at the height of the war effort in 1944 government current expenditure, mainly on military account, had risen to 54·3 per cent of the total as against personal consumption's share of 56·7 per cent. (The expenditure of 111 per cent of net national expenditure during the year was made possible by the run down of fixed assets and borrowing from abroad). With the ending of the war in August 1945, government current expenditure during the year declined in importance to 46·5 per cent of net national expenditure, and this was followed by a much sharper reduction to 25·2 per cent in 1946. From 1944 to 1946 total government current expenditure was cut in current money terms by £2,920 million, or 55·6 per cent, yet net national expenditure as a whole declined by only £434 million, or 4·5 per cent, over this period.

The National Income accounts for the years from 1946 onwards have been drastically revised since the White Paper was published, and this makes direct comparisons with the war years unreliable. However, it is clear from the revised figures that total output, in terms of both current and constant prices, rose in 1947 and again in 1948. The gross domestic product, for example, rose by 6·1 per cent in 1947 and 9·9 per cent in 1948 in terms of current prices, and by 1·3 and 3·3 per cent respectively when measured at constant 1948 prices.

It seems clear from these figures that the disarmament programme after the 1939–1945 war did not lead to more than a minor and short-lived reduction in the total level of economic activity, although in real terms the problem was probably at least three times as great as would be faced now. Moreover, the transition to a mainly non-defence economy took place with considerable speed. In June 1945, after the collapse of Germany, there were some 5·1 million persons in the armed forces backed by approximately 3·9 million persons producing equipment and supplies, giving a total of 9 million persons directly engaged on the defence effort.

In October 1945 a target was set for the demobilisation of 1·5 million men and women from the forces by December 31st, plus a simultaneous reduction of 1·4 million workers in the munitions and related industries. After taking into account those who had already returned to civil life, the achievement of these targets would have meant a reduction of

TABLE 60 *A Breakdown of Net National Expenditure, 1938 to 1946*

	1938		1940		1942		1944		1945		1946	
	£million	per cent	£million	per cent	£million	per cent	£million	per cent	£million	per cent	£million	per cent
Consumption:												
Personal expenditure on consumers' goods and services	4,252	80·4	4,627	67·8	5,133	57·7	5,474	56·7	5,884	61·4	6,584	71·4
Government current expenditure on goods and services	789	14·9	3,213	47·1	4,722	53·1	5,249	54·3	4,450	46·5	2,329	25·2
Additions to assets:												
Net capital formation at home	320	6·0	—212	—3·1	—298	—3·4	—403	—4·2	121	1·3	714	7·7
Net lending abroad and purchases of assets and financial claims from overseas	—70	—1·3	—804	—11·8	—663	—7·4	—659	—6·8	—875	—9·2	—400	—4·3
Net National Expenditure (at market value)	5,291	100·0	6,824	100·0	8,894	100·0	9,661	100·0	9,580	100·0	9,227	100·0

Source: National Income and Expenditure 1938 to 1946, Cmd. 7099.

3,740,000, or 42 per cent, in the manpower engaged on warlike activities, in six months. In the event, despite transport difficulties, the reduction in the armed forces was successfully carried out, and although there appears to have been some shortfall in the industrial field, this is thought to have been due to the failure or inability of some employers to distinguish between defence and non-defence work rather than a failure to meet the target.

The rundown in defence employment was almost complete by the end of 1946. In the Statement Relating to Defence, 1947, Cmd. 7042, published in February, it was stated that 3·5 million persons had been released from the munitions industries and that upwards of 4,290,000 service men and women had been returned to civil life.

The impact of these changes on the total working population was much less than is suggested by the above figures, since during the war years the labour force was swollen by married women and persons past the normal age of retirement, who left the labour force after the cessation of hostilities. Even so, there were considerable changes in the industrial structure of the civil population during the immediate postwar years, and despite the numbers returning from the Services unemployment remained comparatively low[1], as can be seen from the table on page 120.

Over the years 1945 to 1948 the total working population declined by 1,375,000 persons. The numbers in the armed forces fell by 4,244,000 over the same period, while there was an increase of 2,648,000 in the total in civil employment. Of the major industries only the metals, engineering, vehicles and shipbuilding category suffered a large decline in employment, although there was a proportionately greater fall in the numbers employed in the chemicals, explosives, paints, oils etc. industries. Unemployment rose quite substantially over the period as a whole and, in addition, there were 92,000 ex-service men and women not yet in jobs in mid-1948, but, together, they only amounted to 1·8 per cent of the total labour force.

From the viewpoint of both output and employment, therefore, the disarmament programme at the end of the 1939–1945 war was carried out with a minimum of friction and dislocation. Moreover, this transition to a mainly peacetime economy was achieved without the government having to take massive steps to ease the changeover and to support the level of demand. Income taxes were reduced, refunds were made of

---

[1] In February, 1947 the numbers of registered unemployed rose temporarily to nearly 2 million persons, but this was due to the severe weather and the shortage of fuel and power.

TABLE 61 *Changes in the Composition of the Total Working Population, 1945 to 1948*

1945	thousands 1946	1947	1948	Change from 1945 to 1948	
21,649	20,523	20,367	20,274	−1,375	Total working population
14,881	14,638	14,628	14,547	−334	Males
6,768	5,885	5,739	5,727	−1,041	Females
5,090	2,032	1,302	846	−4,244	Total in armed forces and auxiliary services
4,653	1,895	1,238	807	−3,846	Males
437	137	64	39	−398	Females
16,416	17,415	18,650	19,064	+2,648	Total in civil employment
10,133	11,803	13,047	13,437	+3,304	Males
6,283	5,612	5,603	5,627	−656	Females
					of which:
1,041	1,078	1,080	1,123	+82	Agriculture and fishing
799	806	829	839	+40	Mining and quarrying
3,899	3,289	3,485	3,546	−353	Metals, engineering, vehicles and shipbuilding
477	346	356	367	−80	Chemicals, explosives, paints, oils etc.
634	713	783	835	+201	Textiles
481	575	629	613	+132	Clothing, boots and shoes
518	566	609	628	+110	Food, drink and tobacco
159	225	253	263	+104	Cement, bricks, pottery, glass etc.
555	688	768	775	+220	Leather, wood, paper etc.
127	185	218	223	+96	Other manufactures
722	1,184	1,344	1,375	+653	Building and civil engineering
196	240	266	275	+79	Gas, water and electricity supply
1,252	1,367	1,417	1,472	+220	Transport and shipping
1,958	2,170	2,319	2,354	+396	Distributive trades
264	308	347	344	+80	Commerce, banking, insurance and finance
1,903	2,011	2,082	2,128	+225	National and local government
127	88	91	91	−36	Civil Defence, Fire Service and Police
1,334	1,576	1,774	1,813	+479	Miscellaneous services
					Registered insured
103	376	260	272	+169	Unemployed
68	270	193	213	+145	Males
35	106	67	59	+24	Females
40	700	155	92	+52	Ex-members of H.M. forces not yet in employment
27	670	150	90	+63	Males
13	30	5	2	−11	Females

Source: Ministry of Labour, mid-year figures

excess profits taxes, substantial out-payments were made in the form of war damage compensation and a policy of cheap money was adopted, but, for the most part, the government used its very considerable powers during this period to channel demand into particular fields of activity, as there was little need to sustain it. There were, of course, many difficulties experienced during this period, but they were only indirectly attributable to the demobilisation programme. For example, the failure of fuel supplies to meet the demand resulting from the severe weather in 1947, though probably aggravated by the changeover, was certainly not a result of it. Again, although the financial crisis during that year was, without doubt, directly related to the policy of cheap money which was being pursued, this policy was not essential to the demobilisation programme and many observers feel that it actively hindered the return to peacetime conditions.

The explanation of the relative smoothness with which the United Kingdom economy returned to a peacetime basis was the backlog of demand built up during the war years, due both to the devastation and the lack of supplies, coupled with the fact that consumers had the money to translate these demands into actual purchases. The high level of activity during the war and the comparative absence of spending outlets meant that both individual consumers and businesses ended the war with substantial liquid resources, to which the returning servicemen with their gratuities were added. An illustration of how this led to an increase in expenditure out of line with the advance in incomes can be obtained from the following table, which shows the movements in incomes and expenditure from 1938 to 1948. In 1946, for example, disposable incomes rose by only 4·1 per cent, yet consumers' expenditure, measured at market prices, was 21·4 per cent up on 1945. Savings, which had risen to a peak of 22 per cent of disposable income in 1944, fell sharply both in actual terms and as a proportion of income. By 1948, they were down to 1·1 per cent of total disposable income, less than a third of their percentage share in 1938.

American experience after the 1939–1945 war was broadly in line with that of Britain. During the war defence expenditure accounted for over 40 per cent of the gross national product, yet rapid demobilisation was achieved without sizeable unemployment. A full description of American experience after World War II is given in the reply of the Government of the United States of America to the United Nations Economic and Social Council, and published in 'Economic and Social Consequences of Disarmament—Volume II, Replies of Governments

TABLE 62 *Consumers' Income and Expenditure, 1938 to 1948*

£million

	1938	1940	1942	1944	1945	1946	1947	1948
Total private income before tax	4,848	5,815	7,213	8,139	8,400	8,802	9,449	9,963
Direct tax payments	439	585	754	1,123	1,188	1,296	1,295	1,367
Total disposable income	4,409	5,230	6,459	7,016	7,212	7,506	8,154	8,596
Total consumers' expenditure at market prices	4,252	4,627	5,133	5,474	5,884	7,143	7,944	8,505
Savings	157	603	1,326	1,542	1,328	363	210	91

Source: National Income and Expenditure, 1938 to 1946, Cmd. 7099 and National Income Blue Books.

and Communications from International Organisations'. A brief summary is given below.

Defence expenditure by the United States was cut from $145 billion in 1945 to $28 billion in 1946 (in terms of 1960 dollars), whereas over the same period gross private domestic investment increased from $21 billion to $51 billion, consumption from $189 billion to $212 billion, non-defence government expenditure from $19 billion to $27 billion and net exports of goods and services from minus $5 billion to plus $5 billion. Real aggregate demand thus declined by less than half the fall in defence spending, yet over this period over 9 million men were released from the armed forces and unemployment remained below 4 per cent of the labour force.

Four principal factors are listed as having made a major contribution to the ease of the changeover. First, the build up of demand during the war years; second, the fact that both consumers and businesses had accumulated liquid resources which they were quick to translate into purchases; third, the removal of the strain on the labour force caused by the war and the fact that many persons left or voluntarily stayed out of the labour market, and fourth, the spirit of dynamic optimism which prevailed after the war. As in the United Kingdom these factors were reinforced by government policy, principally through tax cuts, transfer payments to war veterans and a government backed veterans' loan programme.

The United States also experienced a period of substantial demobilisation after the Korean War, though the decline in defence expenditure was from a much lower level—from $62 billion in 1953 to $51 billion in 1954 (1960 dollars). Over this period disposable income and consumption both rose, aided by a reduction in tax schedules, and there was also an advance in net exports. This was partly offset by a fall in investment and non-military government expenditure, but the net result was that the GNP declined by less than the reduction in defence spending. Unemployment, however, rose to 5·6 per cent of the labour force, and 1954 is generally considered a recession year.

The United States authorities do not feel that the post-Korean experience is likely to prove typical, as can be seen from the following extract from the American government's reply to the United Nations' enquiry mentioned above.

'Despite the mildness of the 1954 recession it is now clear that fiscal and monetary policies might have been applied with more vigour. The reason they were not is that the decline in defence spending following the Korean War was not treated by the policymakers as a major demobilization requiring strong compensatory action. For this reason the 1953–1954 period does not provide a significant guide to the behaviour of the American economy in a disarmament program during the 1960's.'

Both the United Kingdom's and the United States' experience after the 1939–1945 war clearly indicate that, given the right circumstances, a disarmament programme of considerably greater proportions than would now be necessary can be carried out without causing a major upset to the economy as a whole. When considering the factors that made this possible in both countries, there are two which are of outstanding importance. The first was the backlog of demand built up during the war years as a result of the shortage of supplies and, in the case of the United Kingdom, the destruction of property. The second was that the higher level of activity during the war helped consumers and firms to accumulate reserves which they were eager to translate into purchases of all kinds.

Neither of these factors are present to-day. In the United Kingdom, it is true that savings are running at an unusually high level, but, unlike the wartime situation, this is not due to any lack of spending opportunities. Business profits, on the other hand, have been falling, partly as a result of government measures to restrain demand, and there is some excess capacity in the economy—currently estimated at over 5 per cent of total capacity. Fixed industrial investment seems likely to fall in 1962 as a whole, and although it is expected that investment spending by industry is likely to revive in 1963 it is not foreseen that it will be much greater than the lower level of 1962.

The situation in the United States is in many respects similar, although output has been rising strongly after the recession in 1960 and the early months of 1961. Despite this recovery, confidence that the advance will be maintained is far from strong and unemployment, in the first half of 1962, remained at the high monthly average of $5\frac{1}{2}$ per cent of the labour force. Corporate profits have failed to rise as expected, again partly as a result of excess capacity, so that there seems little likelihood of any significant rise in fixed investment.

In both countries, in contrast to the end-of-the-war feeling of optimism, there appears to be a marked lack of confidence, particularly where businessmen are concerned, in the future. In recent years the growth in output per head of the population was lower in Britain and America than in the other major industrial countries of the world, and means of speeding up the rate of growth are being investigated. In the

United States, a higher rate of growth is, in part, being achieved by allocating larger sums to defence and defence-related expenditure (space research), so that, at the present time, the difficulties likely to be encountered in the event of disarmament are increasing in the United States. This is not true of the United Kingdom—indeed some recent developments have worked in the opposite direction—but defence expenditure rose quite sharply in 1961, and despite the official efforts to economise will almost certainly rise this year and again in 1963.

It seems clear, therefore, that the postwar experience has little direct relevance to present day conditions. This, of course, does not mean that disarmament could not, or should not, be carried out because of the economic difficulties likely to be involved, but that it should be planned to meet the conditions of the day and that these differ widely from those ruling at the end of the war.

Chapter 12

The Period of Transition

As present day conditions vary markedly from those ruling at the time of the postwar disarmament in 1945, it is necessary to consider in greater detail the measures likely to be needed to prevent a programme of disarmament leading to a severe cutback in the overall level of economic activity. At the time of writing, mid-1962, the United Kingdom economy is just starting to advance again after a period of stagnation lasting almost a year. Unemployment at 2·1 per cent of the estimated total number of employees is unusually high by postwar standards, particularly for the time of year, and exceeds unfilled vacancies by a wide margin. Moreover, there are now greater disparities in the regional pattern of unemployment than in May, 1961, as shown in Table 7, page 16, with the position having deteriorated most sharply in the north-west region, Scotland and Wales.

Such factors as these would have to be taken into consideration at the time when a disarmament programme is put into operation, but it should, of course, be recognised that the prevailing conditions may well differ radically from those ruling at the present day. For example, if Britain joins the European Economic Community in the intervening period it might well result in a drastic alteration to the country's economic situation; equally, staying out could have a similarly profound effect. For such reasons, no attempt is made in this chapter to lay down a detailed blue print of the economic measures to be followed in the event of disarmament. Instead, an attempt has been made, in the light of current conditions, to set out in quantitative terms, as far as possible, the size of the problems likely to be faced, to indicate where assistance is most likely to be needed and to assess the costs involved in some of the possible solutions.

THE LENGTH OF THE TRANSITION PERIOD

It was seen in Part I that the direct impact of defence expenditure is concentrated on three broad groups; the armed forces, the service and supply departments of the civil service and the public and private concerns carrying out defence production and research. Within these groups, particularly in the industrial field, certain sectors and individuals are committed on a longer term basis than others. Such factors as, for example, the age and length of engagement of servicemen, the manpower structure of the service and supply departments and the length and extent of individual contracts, would all have to be taken into account in determining the phasing of a disarmament programme from an economic standpoint. Such details, of course, would be known to the government of the day, and it would undoubtedly take them into account when determining the length and speed of a disarmament programme in the light of its political as well as its economic beliefs. Information of this nature is not published in sufficient detail to permit independent researchers to make an accurate appraisal of the situation and, in any event, changes are certain to occur in the future, but given that the length and speed of a disarmament programme must, to a certain extent, be determined by such factors there appears to be some advantage in keeping the transition period as short as possible.

The main reasons for believing this are as follows. First, the quicker the changeover the less is the likelihood that wrong decisions will be made as a result of uncertainty. Second, a much greater psychological impact is likely to be made if the disarmament programme is carried out in the shortest possible time. The third reason, which follows closely from the second, is that people are likely to be much readier to accept the changes involved in a disarmament programme while the agreement itself is still fresh in their memories than after a lapse of a long period of time. Finally, the wasteful use of resources is kept to a minimum if the transition to a fully peacetime economy is carried out in the shortest possible period. (This final reason would not, of course, preclude the temporary continuance of defence projects as a deliberate policy to minimise unemployment).

Because of these factors it seems reasonable to set a two-year period for the transition, although it is clear that many individuals and concerns could change to civil work well within this period and that, in a number of other instances, the changeover might take a longer time.

A two-year transition period is probably the minimum necessary on economic considerations alone. The timing of a disarmament scheme would, of course, be determined mainly by strategic considerations, and it is interesting to note in this respect that the most optimistic scheme yet put forward, from the point of view of timing, envisages a four-year transition period. Since it is clear that a slow rundown of defence expenditure would lead to fewer problems of transition in the economic field than an immediate cut, the following analysis can be considered as covering the shortest possible and most difficult period of transition from an economic point of view.

During the period of transition there could be no question of using the defence expenditures saved for any other purpose than to ease the changeover, and it is probable that an even higher level of expenditure would be required. In addition, the dislocation caused by the transition, and the possible slowing down in the level of activity in related sectors of the economy, could well lead to a loss of revenue through lower tax yields. If this were to occur a clear case would arise for deficit spending (i.e. for current expenditure to exceed current revenue) by the government during this period, in order to counter the multiplier effect of an appreciably lower level of activity in one sector spreading to other sectors, and to offset any lack of confidence in the minds of businessmen and consumers.

In the remainder of this chapter a more detailed examination is made of the three sectors of the economy which would be most affected by disarmament. In so doing, emphasis has been placed on the effects likely to be felt in the United Kingdom itself and by British nationals. It is necessary to limit the analysis in this way both for reasons of time and cost and because of the sheer complexity of the problems likely to be involved on a world-wide scale, but when reading this and the following chapters it is necessary to recognise that similar problems would be faced in many other countries in the west and in the east. Moreover, since the United Kingdom is far from being a closed economy the success or otherwise of its own disarmament programme would necessarily depend, to a certain extent, on the actions of other countries—particularly the United States. Equally, the way in which the British programme is carried out will influence the other countries of the world either for good or ill, and in certain regions of the world the United Kingdom would have special responsibilities because of past military commitments. These extra considerations should always be borne in mind, even when the situation is being considered from a purely British standpoint.

THE ARMED FORCES

There has already been a significant reduction in the numbers in the armed forces since the estimate of total employment on defence at

May, 1961 given in Part I. In the first half of 1962 there were, on average, some 450,000 persons in H.M. Forces and the Women's Services compared with 478,000 in May, 1961. Of this total 433,000 were men and 17,000 were women, and at the end of March, 1962, there were still over 30,000 National Servicemen in the total. In the demobilisation which followed the 1939–1945 war a system of priorities was adopted based on age and length of service. A similar system could be adopted in the event of a disarmament programme, but in the circumstances then ruling it would also be advantageous in arranging the demobilisation to take into account the demand in the civil labour market for the particular skills possessed by servicemen.

The extent to which this will be possible seems likely to be governed by two factors. The first and most important, as was seen above, will be the form of the disarmament agreement itself. It might, for example, lay down the orderly rundown of the armed forces over a period of time during which, in the early stages at least, they would still continue as an efficient, albeit smaller, fighting force. On the other hand, it is possible to envisage an agreement that would permit the rundown of the forces purely in accordance with civil needs, providing that it was carried out within a certain time limit. Although the successful conclusion of a disarmament agreement presupposes a much greater degree of mutual trust than exists at present, it still seems unlikely that, when it is first put into operation, confidence in the integrity of other countries would be sufficient to permit an immediate disbandment of all armed forces. It seems reasonable to assume, therefore, that the armed services would be retained as far as possible as an efficient fighting force during the first stages of any disarmament programme, and that the need to do so would limit the freedom of the administrators to plan the rundown purely in accordance with economic and social considerations.

The second factor which is likely to impose limits on the speed and quality of the demobilisation of the armed forces is the geographical location of the major overseas garrisons. At present, British troops are stationed in large numbers in eleven countries or regions of the world in addition to the United Kingdom and, as at home, the winding up of these overseas garrisons will have to be carried out in cooperation with the local civil authorities. The speed with which this can be accomplished is likely to differ according to the particular circumstances involved and the extent to which the garrison is integrated into the economic life of the community and provides employment for the local people.

Within these limitations, which will gradually be removed with the passage of time if the disarmament agreement is a success, the demobilisation of the forces should be carried out, as far as is otherwise possible, in accordance with the demand for labour in the civil economy. The process of streamlining the Forces which has been under way for a number of years, and is likely to continue, has meant that much greater emphasis has been placed on skill in the Services, and it is skilled labour which is in shortest supply in the labour market. Some of the Service tradesmen would be able to obtain civil jobs with little or no special training; for example, electricians, engineering fitters and mechanics, cooks and clerks. Others, such as armament fitters and mechanics, would almost certainly need training in a civil occupation if the best use were to be made of their skills. Similarly, at the officer level, training would be needed in many instances to fit the persons concerned for managerial and professional jobs in civil life. This could best be carried out while the people concerned were still nominally in the Services, and use made of Service facilities such as lecture rooms, libraries and study rooms. If this were the case the additional cost of the retraining schemes, which might average ten weeks duration, for some 250,000 persons would probably not exceed £100 per head, or a total of £25 million. (This, of course, would not include maintenance which would be covered by the normal Service pay and allowances). The difficulties involved in obtaining suitable teaching staff for such numbers, even if a scheme were adopted of having people on loan from industry for such purposes, would necessarily mean that it would have to be spread over a long period, but an average of 12,500 persons involved at any one period should not prove unworkable.

In addition to helping ex-service personnel to fit themselves for civilian jobs, there is the question of compensation for their early dismissal from the Forces and the loss that this involves. A guide to the type and amount of compensation that should prove adequate can be obtained from the measures adopted at the time of the cuts in Service personnel which began in 1957. A government White Paper, published in 1957, entitled 'Compensation for Premature Retirement from the Armed Forces—Cmnd. 231', gives details of the scheme adopted at that time. In preparing this scheme, four factors of main importance were taken into consideration. These were:—

(a) the curtailment of the expected period of service;
(b) the loss of promotion prospects;
(c) the loss of higher rates of pension which might have been achieved by longer service; and

(d) the additional difficulties in finding employment in civilian life, which may result from the increase in the volume of Service retirements.

All of these would still be relevant, though point (d) is likely to be of greater significance during a period of general disarmament and is, in part, covered by the retraining scheme suggested above.

Outpayments under the scheme were made in accordance with age and length of service, with the highest payments going to the more successful people who had obtained high ranks in the middle of their careers. Those who had completed shorter periods of service, or were nearer to the normal retirement age, received less in the way of additional compensation. Those who were due for retirement in any event, however, received special payments of £500 for officers and £250 for long-service other ranks, to take account of the extra difficulties they would face because their retirement came during the period of a high rate of demobilisation, and a similar scheme would be even more necessary during a general disarmament programme.

The sums paid to officers on premature retirement ranged from a special capital payment of £950 to £6,000 according to rank, age and length of service, plus entitlement to retired pay and terminal grants on a pro rata basis after ten years' service instead of the normal twenty. In the case of other ranks the main emphasis was on mitigating the loss of entitlement to pension through premature retirement. To do this the qualifying period was reduced from twenty-two to ten years' service (after the age of eighteeen), and those who had served over ten years were entitled to add five years to their service for the purposes of calculating their pensions, provided that this did not extend their reckonable service beyond the end of their current engagements. In addition, an extra terminal grant calculated on the same basis was paid plus special capital payments ranging from £250 to £1,250. In the case of both officers and other ranks the special capital payments were tax-free.

Full knowledge of the age, rank and length of service of all Service personnel would be needed to estimate the current cost of putting the scheme into operation, and this is not available. In any case, it would be a fruitless operation to carry out detailed calculations since changes are sure to occur in the future, but a rough guide to the total cost of such a scheme at present can be calculated. For this purpose, a breakdown was obtained from the Ministry of Defence of the numbers of regular officers and other ranks in the Services at the end of March, 1962, with a further breakdown of the male other ranks by length of service engagement.

TABLE 63 *Regular Officers and Other Ranks in the Services at end-March, 1962*

thousands

Men	Women	Total	
52·2	0·9	53·1	Officers
346·3	13·7	360·0	Other ranks of which:
(158·3)	n.a.	n.a.	Up to 9 years engagement[1]
(90·7)	n.a.	n.a.	10–15 years engagement[1]
(78·9)	n.a.	n.a.	Over 15 years engagement[1]
(17·0)	n.a.	n.a.	Boys and apprentices[2]
(1·5)	n.a.	n.a.	Others
398·5	16·8[3]	415·3[3]	Total

[1] These are approximate figures of length of engagement, since the figures were supplied separately for the three Services and they do not use the same time categories. The figures, therefore, provide only a rough guide to the numbers in each category of Service engagement.
[2] Boys and apprentices are not shown separately for the Navy.
[3] Including 2·2 in the Nursing Services.
n.a. Not available.

On the basis of the rates laid down under the 1957 plan, it can be estimated that the capital payments that would have to be paid might average £2,000 per head for officers, £300 per head for other ranks on up to nine year engagements, £1,000 per head for those on ten to fifteen year engagements and £1,500 per head for those with over fifteen years service. For the women's services an average figure of £500 per head has been assumed.

TABLE 64 *An Estimate of Capital Outpayments to the Services in the Event of Disarmament*

£thousands

104,400	Officers—52,200 times £2,000
57,490	Other Ranks—158,300 times £300
90,700	90,700 times £1,000
118,200	78,900 times £1,500
8,400	Women—16,800 times £500
£379,190	Total

In addition to this sum of £380 million, there would be a continuing annual outpayment of service pensions. This is currently running at £60–70 million a year, and might well rise to £110–120 million in the event of disarmament. (On the assumption that an additional 30,000 officers would receive pensions averaging £500 a year and 170,000 men pensions averaging £200 a year).

If the demobilisation of the forces were completed in two years, a total of one year's normal pay and allowances might well have to be paid out during this period, which is currently running at about £350 million. To this would have to be added the £380 million of capital outpayments calculated above, the £25 million for a retraining scheme and the continuing outpayment of a further £50 million a year in pensions after the first year, (this sum would, of course, be gradually reduced with the passage of time). This gives a total sum over a two year period of a little over £800 million compared with a total defence expenditure amounting (at the current rate) to £3,500 million over two years.

THE CIVIL SERVICE

It is clear from the above analysis of the measures likely to be involved in the demobilisation of the members of the armed forces alone—leaving aside for the present the equally, if not more, complicated job of administering the rundown of defence contracts let to industry—that many of the civil servants at present employed in the service and supply departments will be needed to implement the disarmament programme. Even on the assumption of a two-year transition period the work of the administrators could well extend beyond this and into the years ahead, and during the period there would be time for a gradual absorption of personnel into civil departments which might well expand, and for a reduction in the numbers concerned through normal wastage.

The persons to benefit from this job of administration would be those employed at the main administrative centres, particularly London, but the majority of the 200,000 civil servants employed by the service and supply departments in the United Kingdom, approximately 120,000, are employed at Service establishments throughout the country. They fall mainly into two grades, of which the larger is industrial workers (a little over 60,000) and the smaller, clerical workers (55,000).

As was seen in Part I, page 13, it is not possible to make a separate assessment of the prospects for each of the areas of the country where there are Service establishments, and the information obtained in respect of Aldershot and Chatham showed quite clearly the dangers likely to be involved in generalising from particular instances. The best that can be done in a survey of this scale is to point out the problems likely to be involved, and to indicate those sectors which seem likely to be hardest hit.

In this instance it is the industrial workers who will probably find it most difficult to find alternative employment. The greater emphasis on skilled workers in the Services has resulted in larger numbers of civilians being recruited to undertake the less skilled, routine jobs which have to be carried out in all large establishments. Alternative work of this nature, at similar rates of pay, will probably be difficult to find, and the workers concerned are, as a whole, less likely to be suitable for training for more skilled posts. The clerical workers (including typists) are more likely to be able to find other jobs, as there is generally reported to be a shortage of these workers.

In the case of both the industrial grades and the clerical workers, however, and the small numbers of executive and other personnel involved, the problem will be eased by the relatively wide distribution of the Service establishments concerned throughout the country. This should prevent the numbers involved from proving too great a strain on any one area, provided that the problem is recognised in advance and measures taken accordingly. The camps will not all be shut down immediately and this will help to phase the reduction in their civilian labour forces and give time for the workers to look for alternative employment. Those nearing retirement and due for pensions could probably best be catered for by the earlier payment of their pensions when their jobs cease, and those willing and able to train for other posts should receive grants to enable them to do so. By these means it should prove possible to minimise any hardship to those people who are directly employed in these Service establishments.

Of the remaining 80,000 civil servants the majority are in the London area, though it is not possible to locate their place of work with certainty from the information given in the Annual Estimates. A count of those employed by the headquarters of the three main service departments, the Admiralty Office, the War Office and the Air Ministry, gave a total of some 21,650 excluding Service personnel and, where possible, those who worked, or were recruited locally overseas. Over 50 per cent of these, nearly 11,500, were clerical grades and typists, and these grades probably account for an equal proportion of the total of 80,000 civil servants in administrative and technical branches.

After the period of transition the clerical workers and typists who were not absorbed by other government departments would probably have little difficulty in finding alternative work, as there is generally reported to be a considerable shortage of these workers in the London area. Conditions could change, however, and it should be noted that the official figures of unemployment and unfilled vacancies in the Greater London Area do not appear to bear out the general belief of a large unfilled demand. The occupational analysis at June, 1962 showed that 3,715 male clerical workers were unemployed in Greater London against unfilled vacancies totalling only 1,159. In the case of women the official picture is more encouraging with only 1,624 clerical workers unemployed and unfilled vacancies standing at 4,397. It is widely believed that vacancies are not notified to the Exchanges and that the figures do not reflect the true position. This may well be so, but it does seem clear that the position is better for women than for men and that it should not automatically be assumed that vacancies will be available for the persons released by disarmament, or that they will necessarily carry the same pay, conditions of work and pension rights as the Civil Service posts.

Of the other civil servants involved about 1 per cent, or 800, are in the administrative class, 15 per cent, or 12,000, in the executive class, 20 per cent, or 20,000 in the technical grades, 8 per cent, or 6,400 in the industrial grade and the remainder are specialists such as scientists and statisticians. The prospects of some of these finding posts in other government departments, which may well expand in the event of disarmament, must be considered quite good. In the case of the older, more senior staff, early retirement with complete, or nearly complete, pension rights would appear to be the simplest administrative solution, as well as being the most equitable one, on the lines adopted for the armed forces.

Once again, the industrial grades, which are made up of relatively unskilled workers, may constitute a special problem. They consist, for the most part, of paper keepers, messengers, night watchmen and office cleaners, and may prove unsuitable for training for other posts. Many may prefer to retire in the event of their jobs ceasing, and this should help to ease the situation, but some may require special assistance.

In the face of so many unknown factors it is not possible to make any accurate assessment of the numbers likely finally to become redundant in the event of disarmament, as was the case for the armed forces, nor to calculate the order of financial assistance that might prove necessary. On balance, however, it appears from the above analysis that the problem will not be a particularly large one. Government help is likely to be needed in finding alternative employment for the industrial grades and for some of the male clerical workers, and a careful watch will need to be kept to alleviate hardship in individual cases in other grades.

INDUSTRY

Much of the first part of this survey was spent in determining the extent to which industries and firms depend upon defence expenditure. In terms of the numbers employed the three most important industries are aircraft, shipbuilding and electronics, although in proportion to its total employment the ordnance and small arms industry is most heavily engaged on defence work. Within these industries and the others which carry out defence contracts, the extent to which individual firms are involved varies widely, but it was encouraging to note that there is no marked concentration either by size of firms or by the areas of the country in which their defence work is carried out. In terms of the number of workers involved, however, the larger firms predominate and, out of a total of 142 companies the 18 each employing more than 10,000 workers together accounted for three-quarters of the total workers wholly (or mostly) engaged on defence work.

In the period of transition following a disarmament agreement it is clear that in the absence of any positive measures, the ending of defence contracts let to industry would result in short term unemployment as workers became redundant, and that many of the firms concerned would be left with excess capacity and would experience a sharp reduction in turnover and profits. The extent of the unemployment and dislocation would depend, in part at least, on the speed at which the changeover was made, but, as was suggested earlier in this chapter, the advantage appears to lie in keeping the transition period as short as possible. A further factor in support of this contention, with special reference to industry, is that a delay in helping one industry which is likely to be adversely affected, may well prevent related industries from making adjustments which they would otherwise be willing to make and capable of carrying out.

Moreover, it should not be assumed that changes of this nature are unusual or unwelcome in the normal course of events, although they usually occur on a smaller scale. Shifts in the pattern of employment and the use of financial resources are inevitable if the economy is to keep pace with new developments, and it is customary for large numbers of people to change their jobs during the course of the year. In the twelve months ending June, 1962, for example, the total of persons in civil employment rose by only 70,000, yet there were nearly 1·9 million vacancies filled during the period. Most of the changes of employment involve a move to another job in the same or a similar industry, but there is also a growing movement across industry boundaries. In some cases, the reason for the change of jobs is simply the attraction of better pay or working conditions, but in others it is declining employment opportunities in a particular industry which forces people to seek alternative employment. The cotton industry is an example of the latter case, and similar prospects now face some of the workers in the railway and coal industries.

It is not surprising, therefore, in the light of such developments and of the government's policy of maintaining full employment, that there is already a wide range of measures in force designed to alleviate the hardships of the unemployed and to assist them to find new work. In the first instance there is, of course, the payment of unemployment benefits to workers for both themselves and their dependents, under the National Insurance Scheme, where unemployment is unavoidable. The second major means of combatting unemployment is the Employment Exchange Service, which is designed to bring employment opportunities to the notice of those seeking work, and to fit them into suitable jobs with the minimum of delay.

Measures to assist local unemployment can be taken under the Local Employment Act, 1960, which is administered by the Board of Trade. It can designate as 'development districts' areas where high unemployment exists or is expected, and can offer a wide range of inducements to industrialists to expand or to establish themselves in these areas. Where no work is available in their home area, unemployed persons who obtain work in other districts can obtain assistance under the Ministry of Labour Transfer Schemes, and retraining facilities are available at Government Training Centres.[1] Training allowances for workers were increased in September, 1962, to £7 10s. a week for a man aged over 21 without dependents, to £8 10s. for a man with a dependent wife and to £9 for a man with a dependent wife and two or more dependent children. Lodging allowances payable under transfer schemes were also increased from 35s. to 42s. a week.

---

[1] At present there are 13 such centres, 11 in England and one each in Scotland and Wales. The number of places available totals 2,450, of which 1,870 were taken up at the end of June, 1962. In the event of disarmament this scheme would undoubtedly have to be expanded.

Industry itself has also taken steps to meet this problem, and a growing number of firms now operate redundancy schemes under which payments are made to redundant workers in accordance with their previous wage rates and length of service. The desire to remove opposition to change is one reason for the adoption of such schemes, and the issues involved have been studied on a national level through the British Employers' Confederation and the Trades Union Congress.

All such measures, and the above list is not exhaustive, can be used to alleviate the problems likely to face industry in the event of a transition from a partly defence to a purely civil economy. Because of the size and complexity of the operation, however, some special measures are also likely to be needed to deal with the difficulties of particular industries and sectors of industries, and in the remainder of this chapter an attempt is made to show which industries are likely to be concerned and to suggest ways by which their difficulties can best be overcome.

The industrial sector directly controlled by the government is one that is almost certain to require special treatment in the event of disarmament. For security reasons it was not possible to visit any establishments such as the Royal Ordnance Factories or Naval Dockyards, but between them they probably employ between 50,000 and 60,000 workers. Moreover, in the case of the Naval Dockyards, it is common knowledge that these are concentrated in a few regions of the country, and it can be seen from Appendix A that one such region, Chatham, is already an area of high unemployment.

It is difficult to envisage, in the event of disarmament, that alternative government employment would be available for the workers in these establishments, unless the government of the day takes a policy decision to enter the field of general manufacturing industry. Even if this were the case the Naval Dockyards would almost certainly still be in difficulties, since their only suitable alternative employment would appear to be merchant shipbuilding—an industry which is already depressed and one which is likely to be further adversely affected by general disarmament. For the areas which rely on government establishments of this nature for a significant proportion of their total employment, there would appear to be a clear case, therefore, for the Board of Trade to use its powers to attract new industry into the regions. This would have to be allied with a government sponsored retraining scheme and, possibly, grants to workers prepared to move to other areas to obtain new jobs.

In the case of private industry it would not be unreasonable to expect the more prosperous firms, and those capable of finding alternative outlets for their products, to bear at least part of the costs involved in any transition. Nearly all the firms interviewed, however, stressed the need for adequate warning if they were successfully to help themselves carry out the changeover, and most felt that when changes had occurred in the past insufficient warning had been given. As it seems unlikely that there will be a sudden conclusion of a disarmament treaty this should prove possible, and a period of at least six months' warning of a withdrawal of defence contracts ought to provide sufficient time for the majority of firms concerned to assesss the problems likely to be involved and to prepare estimates of the redundancy, if any, that would result.

Armed with this information the rundown of defence contracts could be co-ordinated and planned to run concurrently with the measures being taken to provide alternative employment and not, as appears to have happened in the past, for the two to be run successively and planned quite independently. For instance, if, as was suggested at a number of the interviews with companies, defence spending on military aircraft and rockets were to be in part replaced by a civil space research pro-gramme, it would clearly minimise the problems of transition if the new contracts were phased, as far as is practical, to coincide with the running out of defence contracts.

Even if this and similar schemes were possible, it still seems likely that there would be unemployment in the aircraft and shipbuilding industries, where competition for civil markets is already intense and where it will almost certainly increase in the event of disarmament. In these industries, and in others where companies are prepared to diver-sify into new fields, government grants towards the cost of re-equip-ment, possibly related to the numbers to be employed, could be given during the period when defence contracts were running out. In the case of the less seriously affected firms, these grants could be replaced by special investment allowances for new equipment and by accelerated depreciation allowances for obsolete defence machinery. Such measures should be accompanied by retraining schemes, where necessary, for the workers concerned, to be carried out whenever possible in the companies' own premises. According to the extent and nature of the training to be given, government grants could be paid to workers in place of a part or the whole of their normal wages, up to the amounts allowed for workers retraining at the Government Training Centres.

Such measures, allied with the existing facilities for dealing with redundancy and unemployment, should go a long way to meet the problems resulting from the ending of defence expenditure in the production field, but this would still leave the problem of defence financed research. Both the government and private industry are directly concerned in defence research, although the number of workers involved is likely to be greater in the private sector. It was shown in Part I that some £240 million was spent on defence research in 1960–61, exclusive of an undisclosed amount in the atomic field. Of this total about £47 million went on basic and applied research, carried out almost entirely by government departments, and £190 million went on development, about £175 million of which was spent with industry.

The results of basic research in the defence field need not necessarily be of value to defence alone, and some may be worth continuing for their possible civil applications. In respect of the other projects it should be relatively simple, within the limits of technical feasibility, to transfer the resources and expenditure to civil research, possibly under the control of the D.S.I.R. or the civil branch of the Ministry of Aviation, instead of the service and supply departments. Similarly, the scope for civil research projects in the atomic energy field is almost certainly sufficient to take up any slack left by the ending of defence expenditure, once again providing that the changeover is technically possible.

The defence research carried out by industry is mainly concerned with development and, in part at least, it is difficult to distinguish from production. One of the main problems likely to arise in the event of defence expenditure ceasing is the shortage of work for the technically qualified staff that are the basis of individual research teams. It was stressed by companies during the interviews that much of the value of a research team lies in its corporate entity rather than in the skills of its individual members, and that much of value to the future growth and development of the economy would be lost if these research teams were allowed to be disbanded.

One method of keeping them together would be by increasing the government contribution to the cooperative research at present carried out by industry research associations. In 1961, D.S.I.R. grants to the separate industry research associations, and those serving industry as a whole, totalled £1·97 million, compared with the £175 million that went to industry in the form of defence research contracts. The selection of cooperative research projects could be left to the industries concerned, and these would be financed entirely by grants from the government. In contrast to the present practice the actual research, in the first instance at least, could be carried out by companies within the industry that have unemployed research facilities, and this should go a long way towards holding the nucleus of research teams together as well as providing a stimulus to privately financed research by the companies concerned.

The scope for encouraging private research would, in the circumstances, probably be more limited than is the case for production. The accelerated depreciation allowances, plus the investment allowances, already permit four-fifths of the capital invested in research to be written off in the first year of its life, and any further incentive of this nature is unlikely to prove very attractive at a time when profits are in decline or losses are being made. There is, however, already a movement towards sponsoring civil research projects through the National Research and Development Council, and this could well be expanded by a system of loans and grants. In the first instance, the emphasis could best be placed on direct grants to cover part or the whole of the research costs of projects that seem likely to lead to increased production and employment in the future. At a later stage, a system of loans to be repaid when projects come to fruition would probably be more suitable.

In the preceding paragraphs no attempt has been made to lay down a detailed course of action for meeting the problems likely to be faced by industry in the event of disarmament. Instead, attention has been drawn to the considerable administrative apparatus that already exists to deal with such problems, and to indicate the points at which it might need supplementing. The extent of the extra help needed would largely depend on how far the government is able to maintain its total level of expenditure during the period and thus to instil a spirit of confidence in the persons and companies affected. There is certain to be considerable need for consultation with the industries and the trade unions concerned, both to explain government policy and to minimise the possibility of misunderstandings occurring, and to seek their help in finding workable solutions. Some change from the existing pattern is inevitable if any benefit is to be reaped from disarmament, and if it can be ensured that the gains will not take too long to materialise and that the interests of individuals will be safeguarded in the interim period, the transition period should pass without any major setback being experienced by the economy as a whole.

Chapter 13

The Ending of the Transition Period;
Forecasts of the Permanent Redistribution
of Expenditure

As has been shown in the previous chapter, in order to avoid the danger of a recession developing from the multiplier effects of a sudden ending of any substantial part of the defence programme, a carefully planned period of transition of at least two years would be essential. During this period the government should, if necessary, undertake deficit spending to mount the programme for the re-allocation of expenditure before cuts in defence spending take their effect on incomes and profits.[1] Only if there is some overlapping in the phasing of these two operations will the revenues at present corresponding to defence spending gradually become available over time to build up a budget for other purposes. Any precipitate cutting of defence spending or any out of phase component in the transition programme leading to a fall in total expenditure of the order, for example, of £200–300 million would result in a significant fall in economic activity, business confidence and government revenue which, in the circumstances of disarmament, might prove extremely hard to regain.

It should not be expected, therefore, that the total amount currently being spent on defence, or on easing the period of transition, would cease at any one point of time. The need to replace defence expenditure by civil expenditure would be a gradual process, and only after a number of years would the total sum now spent on defence projects cease completely. When considering alternative types of expenditure it is essential to bear this reservation in mind. Equally, not all forms of expenditure are capable of being put into practice immediately—this is particularly true of most forms of capital expenditure—so that when

---

[1] The need for deficit spending will depend on the size of the above-the-line budget surplus. For the financial year 1962–63, this is estimated at £443 million.

considering alternatives to defence spending there may well be a conflict, in the short term, between the overall desirability and the immediate suitability of particular items of expenditure. This is mainly a question of advance planning, and does not constitute any long term bar to the adoption of particular forms of expenditure.

As was the case during the period of transition the essential point is to replace the defence expenditure by an equal quantity of non-defence expenditure, in order to prevent a fall in total output, and the amount of defence expenditure to be replaced may be expected eventually to build up to £1,500 million a year. Since the government directly controls this expenditure, it would be possible for it simply to replace the amount it spends on defence by other current purchases of goods and services, but for both political and economic reasons it is unlikely to do so. It is much more likely to make up part of the deficiency by using its powers to stimulate other forms of expenditure, both in the public and the private sphere.

For illustrative purposes it has been assumed that the defence expenditure will be replaced in three equal parts by private consumption expenditure, capital or investment expenditure and by government current expenditure. This final category has been further sub-divided into two; current purchases of goods and services by public authorities and aid to underdeveloped countries. In the first instance, of course, aid will appear as a transfer payment, but it has been assumed for the purposes of this illustration that it is fully reflected in increased expenditure on exports. By the means of this hypothetical breakdown it is possible to trace the likely effects of these different forms of expenditure on the economy as a whole, and in later chapters to relate them to the estimated costs of implementing particular forms of expenditure.

An indication of the significance to the various sectors of the economy of a redistribution of £1,500 million in this fashion can be obtained from the national expenditure figures for 1961. It would mean an increase of £500 million each in consumers' expenditure and in gross fixed capital formation at home, and a net reduction of £1,250 million in public authorities' current expenditure. In total, this would result in a fall of £250 million in total domestic expenditure, which would be offset by higher exports, leaving the gross national product unchanged. It would not, of course, be possible to make changes on this scale during any one year, but the calculations which are set out in Table 65 give a clear indication of the magnitude of the changes involved.

TABLE 65 *An Illustration, using the 1961 Figures, of One Method of Replacing Defence Expenditure by the Main Types of Civil Expenditure*

Expenditure in 1961	Changes in expenditure which could result from disarmament	Revised expenditure on the basis of the 1961 figures	Expenditure generating gross national product
			At market prices:
17,302	+500	17,802	Consumers' expenditure
4,596[1]	−1,250	3,346	Public authorities' current expenditure on goods and services
			Gross fixed capital formation at home:
820 ⎱	500	910	Dwellings
3,710 ⎰		4,120	Other
273	nil	273	Value of physical increase in stocks and work in progress
26,701	−250	26,451	Total domestic expenditure at market prices
6,754	+250	7,004	Exports and income received from abroad
−6,715	nil	−6,715	less Imports and income paid abroad
−3,635	nil	−3,635	less Taxes on expenditure
598	nil	598	Subsidies
23,703	nil	23,703	Gross national expenditure at factor cost (gross national product)

[1] Defence expenditure is included in this figure.

An extra £500 million, in terms of 1961 prices, would raise consumers' expenditure in 1961 to £17,802 million, or by 2·9 per cent. Current expenditure on goods and services by the public authorities would fall by a net amount of £1,250 million, or by 27·2 per cent, but the £250 million increase in their civil expenditure would represent an increase of 8·7 per cent on the 1961 figures. Gross fixed capital formation, at £5,030 million, would be 11 per cent higher than it was in 1961, and the net result of all these changes would be to reduce total domestic expenditure by 0·4 per cent. This would be offset by the increase of £250 million, or 3·7 per cent, in exports, to leave the gross national product unchanged.

Tables 66, 67, and 68 show in greater detail the effects that a redistribution of defence expenditure could have on the domestic economy, using the pattern of expenditure in 1961 as a guide. In each case it has been assumed that the total increase in each category is distributed in proportion to the importance of each main type of expenditure in 1961. In fact, it is very unlikely that the money would be spent in this fashion. In the case of consumers' expenditure, for example, after a certain level of expenditure has been reached, the proportion of each increment of income which is spent on necessities such as food tends to decrease, so that it is unlikely, providing that the extra £500 million is spent by consumers in general, that foodstuffs will account for as high a proportion of an extra £500 million as they do of total consumers' expenditure.[1] Of course, the actual way in which an extra £500 million is spent by consumers would depend to a very great extent upon which group of consumers does the spending, and this and other factors are considered in greater detail in the following chapters. The calculations shown in the tables do, however, provide a guide to the type and the extent of the opportunities that would arise in the event of disarmament.

It is, of course, extremely unlikely that the changes set out in Table 65 could occur without leading to alterations in other sectors of the economy. For example, part of the extra consumers' expenditure is likely to go on items which are subject to purchase tax, and since little, if any, of the direct defence expenditure would be of this nature, it is reasonable to assume that taxes on expenditure would increase if the rates of tax remained unaltered, so that more than £500 million of extra expenditure would be required. In addition, the import content of defence expenditure is unlikely to be exactly matched by that of the civil expenditure which replaces it, and this would again lead to a change in the gross national product as a whole.

Sufficient knowledge of the working of the economy is not yet available to make accurate predictions of the consequences of reactions such as these, although an attempt has recently been made by the Department

[1] Engel's Law: as income rises the proportion spent on food declines.

TABLE 66 *The Effect on the Main Types of Consumers' Expenditure in 1961 of a Total Increase of £500 million*[1]

Consumers' expenditure at current prices 1961	Increases which could result from disarmament	Revised consumers' expenditure on the basis of the 1961 figures	
4,989	144	5,133	Food
			Alcoholic drink:
618	18	636	Beer
433	13	446	Other
1,218	35	1,253	Tobacco
1,599	46	1,645	Housing
793	23	816	Fuel and light
			Durable goods:
386	11	397	Furniture and floor coverings
384	11	395	Radio and electrical goods, etc.
516	15	531	Cars and motor cycles
			Clothing:
299	8	307	Footwear
1,388	40	1,428	Other
2,124	62	2,186	Other goods
2,555	74	2,629	Other services
17,302	500	17,802	Total

[1] Distributed in proportion to the importance of each type of expenditure in 1961.

of Applied Economics at Cambridge University[1] to build a model that would make it possible to do so. This model was used by the British Government in the preparation of its reply for the United Nations Survey of the Economic and Social Consequences of Disarmament, in order to make 'an assessment of the implications of replacing defence expenditure in equal parts by consumption, by capital formation (of the same composition as the increase in capital formation between 1955 and 1960) and by foreign aid (of the same commodity composition as

[1] An account of the work carried out to date is given in a paper entitled 'A Computable Model of Economic Growth' by Richard Stone and Alan Brown, published for the Department of Applied Economics, University of Cambridge, by Chapman and Hall.

TABLE 67 *The Effect on Public Authorities' Expenditure in 1961 of an Ending of Defence Expenditure and an increase of £250 million[1] in Civil Expenditure*

Public authorities' current expenditure in 1961	Changes which could result from disarmament	Revised expenditure by public authorities on the basis of the 1961 figures	
			Central government: Current expenditure on goods and services:
1,735	−1,500	235[2]	Military defence
801	+70	871	Health services
564	+49	613	Other
3,100	−1,381	1,719	Total
			Local authorities Current expenditure on goods and services:
740	+65	805	Education
756	+66	822	Other
1,496	+131	1,627	Total
4,596	−1,250	3,346	Combined total

[1] Distributed in proportion to the importance of each type of civil expenditure in 1961.
[2] This expenditure would eventually disappear.

United Kingdom exports in 1959 to Commonwealth countries) made available for transfer by direct gift overseas.'

The results of this calculation are subject to a number of important qualifications. In calculating the role of defence expenditure, for example, it was assumed that military products and the total products of each industry concerned require the same inputs from other industries, but because of the greater proportion of research contracts in military work its input of materials and imports is likely to be lower than the average. The calculations, therefore, may tend to overstate the relative importance of the indirect contribution to defence production and research and of its import content. Another important qualification is

TABLE 68 *The Effect on the Main Types of Capital Expenditure in 1961 of a Total Increase of £500 Million*[1]

Gross fixed capital formation at home at current prices in 1961	Increase which could result from disarmament	Revised gross fixed capital formation on the basis of the 1961 figures	
			Analysis by industry group:
102	11	113	Mining and quarrying
1,274	141	1,415	Manufacturing
447	50	497	Gas, electricity and water
516	57	573	Transport and communication[2]
853	94	947	Distribution and other industries[2]
820	90	910	Dwellings
461	51	512	Public services
57	6	63	Legal fees, etc.
4,530	500	5,030	Total
			Analysis by type of asset:
633	70	703	Vehicles, ships and aircraft
1,702	188	1,890	Plant and machinery
820	90	910	Dwellings
1,375	152	1,527	Other new buildings and works[3]
4,530	500	5,030	Total
			Analysis by sector:
			Public
282	31	313	Dwellings
1,513	167	1,680	Other
			Private:
538	59	597	Dwellings
2,197	243	2,440	Other
4,530	500	5,030	Total

[1] Distributed in proportion to the importance of the main types of capital expenditure in 1961.
[2] Road goods transport is included with distribution, not with transport.
[3] Including legal fees, etc.

that the model from which the calculations were produced has not demonstrated that the extra capital resources made available by disarmament will match the requirements of the expanding industries.

The table below sets out the results of the calculation, in the form of percentage changes required in the net outputs of the main industry groups concerned. As would be expected, the largest change is a reduction of some 20 per cent in the net output of the omnibus industry group, ships, railway vehicles and aircraft. The net output of every other

TABLE 69 *Differences between Net Outputs (by Industrial Sectors) required respectively with 1959 Military Expenditure and with this replaced by Extra Consumption, Extra Fixed Capital Formation and Extra Foreign Aid (in Equal Parts)*

Difference in £ million, 1959	Difference as a % of g.n.p.	Difference as a % of sector net output	Sector
+30	+0·2	+3·5	1A. Agriculture
+33	+0·2	+4·0	1B. Food
+38	+0·2	+4·1	2. Coal etc.
+20	+0·1	+6·0	3. Clothing
+96	+0·5	+4·6	4. Engineering
+11	+0·1	+5·6	5. Wood
+47	+0·3	+8·7	6. Textiles
+59	+0·3	+13·9	7. Motors
+27	+0·2	+3·5	8. Other manufacturing
+42	+0·2	+2·6	9. Transport
+84	+0·4	+7·1	10. Buildings
			11. Services
−547	−2·7	−100	(a) Military
+24	+0·3	+0·5	(b) All other
+19	+0·1	+3·5	12. Gas, water, electricity
+33	+0·1	+5·2	13. Chemicals
+43	+0·2	+6·4	14. Metals
−124	−0·6	−19·8	15. Ships, railway vehicles and aircraft
+126	+0·3	+4·9	16. Distribution
−42			17. Imports

Source: United Nations—Economic and Social Consequences of Disarmament, Volume II—Replies of Governments and Communications from International Organisations.

industry group is expanded, mostly by between 3 and 6 per cent, and by nearly 14 per cent in the motor industry. The report also states that about 3½ per cent of the occupied population would be required to cross the boundaries of industry groups as a result of these changes.

No attempt has been made to make similar calculations for this survey, and since it would have been necessary to use the Cambridge model to make the calculations the results, apart from the different assumptions used, are not likely to have differed very greatly from those given in the table above. The probable consequences of an addition of an extra £500 million to consumers' disposable income have instead been predicted to a certain extent from present trends in the pattern of expenditure both in this country and in the United States, and the different effects of various methods of distributing the extra money to consumers, through cuts in the standard rate of income tax, discriminatory tax allowances or purchase tax relief, are also considered. The ways in which increased old age pensions, unemployment benefits or government salaries would be spent are much more difficult to predict than an increase in consumers' expenditure as a whole, and the effects of these changes in transfer payments on the economy is correspondingly difficult to forecast. Increased unemployment benefits, however, can be a means of encouraging labour mobility between industries and areas, which would be of great importance for some years after disarmament. Larger contributions to the developing countries could be a means of providing British industries with new export markets, but could also have serious effects upon the balance of payments; these consequences would again depend upon the means by which aid was distributed.

The chapter on increased investment covers both directly productive (endogeneous) and social and other (exogenous) investment. An increase in directly productive investment would be of primary importance to the economy; although British industry still has a high level of capital equipment employed per man, the proportion of national income invested in capital equipment in recent years has been appreciably lower than in the countries of the European Economic Community. Social investment as a whole is of equally great importance, but has a longer term influence upon the economy. Investment in education is believed to be a major factor in influencing economic growth, and in the field of higher education in particular Britain is again well behind her European competitors. Investment in roads has been classified as social investment, although it can be very closely related to production.

It must be emphasised that the division of expenditure is in no way a recommended pattern; the particular projects investigated have been selected quite arbitrarily as a means of illustrating the range of possibilities that would arise in the event of disarmament. The extent to which they would require the use of the same amount of revenue as was needed for defence expenditure will depend both on the type of expenditure and the way in which it is induced. It is theoretically possible, for example, for an extra £1,500 million of investment expenditure to be induced purely by monetary measures, and this would leave the whole of the revenues currently spent on defence free for other uses. On the other hand, as is shown in Chapter 14, because of the growing tendency of consumers to save a high proportion of any additional income which they receive, in the case of consumers' expenditure it might well be necessary to use a significantly greater sum of revenue to induce expenditure of £500 million. For the purposes of this analysis, however, the cost to the revenue of inducing civil expenditure to replace defence expenditure is of secondary importance, since provided that the extra expenditure is forthcoming, no matter how it is financed, it will prevent any downturn in the economy as a whole, which must be the main objective of any economic disarmament programme.

Chapter 14

The Redistribution of Defence Expenditure to Private Consumption

THE PRESENT PATTERN OF CONSUMERS' EXPENDITURE AND THE EFFECTS OF AN INCREASE FROM DEFENCE REVENUE

Total personal disposable income after tax in the United Kingdom in 1961 amounted to £19,374 million, of which £17,302 million was spent. The average real rate of growth (i.e. at constant 1954 prices) of total disposable income over the last five years has been 4·1 per cent, while the average real rate of growth of consumers' expenditure has been 2·2 per cent.

TABLE 70 *Consumer Income and Expenditure, 1957-1961*

Total personal disposable income (current prices) [£million]	Rate of growth (constant 1954 prices) [%]	Consumers' expenditure (current prices) [£million]	Rate of growth (constant 1954 prices) [%]	
15,450		14,477		1957
16,074	1·2	15,221	2·3	1958
16,933	4·8	15,921	4·1	1959
18,207	6·7	16,613	3·5	1960
19,374	3·5	17,302	1·4	1961

Source: Central Statistical Office.

In the event of disarmament an increase in consumers' expenditure would be an obvious means of replacing a proportion of the demand arising from defence. The addition of, for example, £500 million to the total of personal disposable income for 1961 would represent an increase of 2·6 per cent, and if the whole sum were spent it would increase 1961 expenditure by 2·9 per cent. The impact of a sum of this size would therefore in ordinary circumstances be of small importance, although if it were given to consumers in a year like 1960, in which the natural growth of income was exceptionally high, or in a year like 1958, in which it was exceptionally low, an existing trend could be heavily accentuated or alternatively counteracted. Its impact in the circumstances of disarmament would however be of considerable importance, as part of the general necessity to ensure that the whole demand for goods and services at present arising from defence would be replaced. The particular effects, moreover, if expenditure were concentrated in a few sectors only, could be much more sharply felt.

If the additional £500 million were distributed to consumers in general through measures of income tax relief, however, it is probable that consumers would decide to save a proportion of the addition to their incomes. Personal savings are now on a scale which makes it theoretically possible for consumers to save the whole of an increase of this size in their incomes; the increase in personal savings in 1960, for example, was greater than £500 million, and the 1961 increase was almost as large.

TABLE 71 *Personal Savings, 1957–1961*

Personal savings (current prices) (£ million)	Personal savings as a % of total disposable income	
973	6·3	1957
853	5·3	1958
1,012	6·0	1959
1,594	8·8	1960
2,072	10·7	1961

Source: Central Statistical Office.

The average marginal propensity to save over the last ten years, however, has been 0·3. The sharp increase in 1960 can be partly accounted for by official discouragement of consumers' expenditure, particularly through hire purchase restrictions, and to this extent consumers would be less likely to save the addition to their incomes if it were distributed at a time when restrictions were relaxed. It can nevertheless also be argued that as consumers become more prosperous they will choose to devote a higher proportion of income to life assurance and other forms of saving, and that this new trend towards a higher rate of saving may be a permanent one. American experience tends to contradict this belief, since personal savings in the U.S. in 1960 amounted to 6·5 per cent of personal disposable income, as compared to 8·8 per cent in the U.K. American savings per head, however, stood at £45, having fallen from over £50 in 1960, while savings per head in the U.K. stood at £30 in 1960 and rose to just over £39 in 1961. A further increase of some £300 million would have been needed in 1961 in order to bring savings per head to the American level for 1960.

On the assumption that the average marginal propensity to save of the last ten years would operate in the year in which the additional £500 million were distributed, the amount saved would be in the region of £150 million and the amount spent in the region of £350 million. The main purpose of redistributing defence expenditure to consumers would to some extent be defeated, since the whole of the demand arising from this proportion of defence expenditure would not be replaced. If it had been decided, therefore, that exactly £500 million of defence demand should be replaced by demand for consumer goods and services, and that this demand should be stimulated by means of tax reliefs, it would be necessary for the government to forego some £710 million in revenue in order to make sure that consumers' expenditure rose by £500 million.

The existing pattern of consumers' expenditure gives some indication of how consumers would choose to distribute a total increase between the various categories of demand.

Table 72 shows a breakdown of consumers' expenditure at constant prices for the years 1957, 1959 and 1961. It can be seen that in recent years consumers have chosen to allot a declining proportion of their total expenditure to food and housing. Total expenditure on each of these has risen since 1957, but only by 6·6 per cent in the case of food and by 5·2 per cent in the case of housing, whereas total consumers' expenditure rose by nearly 12 per cent.

Spending on clothing has risen slightly as a percentage of total expenditure, and more sharply as a total than either food or housing. Expenditure on the whole category of durable goods has risen sharply both as a percentage of total expenditure and in total value, although its rate of growth has slowed down in recent years. Spending on cars and motor cycles has risen particularly fast, total expenditure having increased by 65 per cent between 1957 and 1961. Spending on radio and electrical goods declined between 1959 and 1961, but was still 16 per cent higher than in 1957.

A comparison of the British figures with a recent breakdown of consumers' expenditure in the United States indicates no very marked

TABLE 72 *Trends in Consumers' Expenditure, 1957–1961*

In the United Kingdom (average 1958 prices)

		Durable goods							
Food	Housing[1]	Furniture	Radio and[2] electrical etc.	Cars and[2] motor cycles	Clothing	Other goods[3]	Other services	Total expenditure	
4,574	1,336	233	346	331	1,450	4,217	2,286	14,873	1957 £million
30.8	9.0	2.2	2.3	2.2	9.7	28.4	15.4	100	per cent
4,721	1,368	391	449	544	1,512	4,542	2,318	15,845	1959 £million
29.8	8.6	2.5	2.8	3.4	9.5	28.7	14.7	100	per cent
4,879	1,406	366	402	548	1,644	4,981	2,392	16,618	1961 £million
29.4	8.5	2.2	2.4	3.3	9.9	29.9	14.4	100	per cent

Source: Central Statistical Office

In the United States[4]

Food	Housing[1]	Furniture	Radio and[2] electrical etc.	Cars and[2] motor cycles	Clothing	Other goods[3]	Other services	Total expenditure	
21.3	13.9	2.6	2.5	4.8	8.6	21.6	24.5[5]	100	1960 per cent

Source: U.S. Department of Commerce: Survey of Current Business

[1] Rent, rates, water charges, repairs.
[2] Including non-electrical household appliances such as lawn mowers, pedal cycles etc.
[3] Including fuel and light.
[4] Definitions are not exactly similar, but have been made to coincide as far as possible.
[5] Medical and dental services 4.4 per cent.

differences at a higher level of consumer income. Spending on food constitutes a still smaller proportion of total expenditure in the United States, but spending on housing a larger one; expenditure on furniture and electrical goods constitutes a similar proportion of income in both countries, but expenditure on cars is larger in the United States. The proportion of an American consumer's income spent on services is considerably higher than that of the British consumer, even allowing for the necessity to spend on medical care in the U.S.

A sum equal to one-third or even one-half of defence expenditure is not large enough to raise consumers' income to a significantly higher level, and would therefore be unlikely to alter existing trends in expenditure. If it were added to consumer incomes at a point in the course of the next few years, therefore, and assuming that the increase were distributed according to the existing pattern of incomes, the largest percentage increases in expenditure could be expected in the durable goods categories. Some of the additional spending would of course go to non-durable goods, such as food and clothing, and total expenditure on these two items is so large than an increase even of 1 to 2 per cent could account for 18 to 36 per cent of the proposed addition to expenditure. Increased spending on food in this country in recent years has been attributable to purchases of more expensive foods rather than to larger quantities; expenditure on the 'convenience' foods has risen in particular, and is now estimated as being in the region of £900 million a year, of which about half consists of tinned and frozen foods. As a proportion of total expenditure on food this is still below the U.S. level; annual consumption of frozen food, for example, amounts to some 6 pounds per head in the U.K. and to some 40 pounds per head in the U.S. The British market for frozen foods, currently estimated at £57 million a year, has been growing at the rate of 20 per cent per annum. If consumers chose to increase their spending on all convenience foods by 5 per cent, this could account for some £45 million of extra income, but imported foods would probably benefit from at least 25 per cent of this additional expenditure.

It may be assumed, however, that unless this increment were distributed to consumers at a time of general restrictions on expenditure, the largest increases in demand would probably arise in the durable goods categories, and would consequently mainly benefit domestic manufacturers. Increased spending on motor vehicles would be particularly important. The average number of persons per car in the U.K. at the end of 1960 was 9·3, as compared with 2·9 in the U.S.; geographical differences make this comparison to some extent unrealistic, but there is nevertheless considerable room for expansion of ownership, which could be encouraged if, as seems likely, road building were included in a post-disarmament investment programme. Purchase tax relief could have an immediate effect on the demand for cars; income tax relief would have a delayed effect, since it would not affect the size of the necessary hire purchase deposit, although it would reduce the time necessary to save it. The amount of additional expenditure on motor vehicles is difficult to predict; the largest growth in expenditure so far experienced in this sector in any one year was the rise of £114 million (at constant 1958 prices) in 1959. This was largely attributable to the relaxation of hire purchase restrictions, although total disposable income also grew in that year by more than the average annual amount. An appreciable cut in purchase tax might result in a growth in expenditure in any one year of a sum of this order, some proportion of this increase being due to the natural growth of the market rather than to this particular factor.

Among other durable consumer goods, a comparison of ownership figures here and in the United States seems to indicate that expenditure would be most likely to increase on refrigerators and washing machines and the smaller electrical appliances.

TABLE 73 *Estimates of the Percentage of Households Owning Certain Electrical Consumer Goods in the United Kingdom and the United States*

End 1961		
United Kingdom	United States	
75	89	Television
76	94	Radio
28	98	Refrigerator
40	96	Washing machine
74	76	Vacuum cleaner
5	58	Food and drink mixer
12	81	Toaster

Radio and television markets now consist mainly of replacement demand, although the advent of mass-produced colour television sets could radically alter the situation. Home sales of radios, radiograms and television sets in 1961 amounted to £75 million; television sales alone reached a peak of £94 million in 1959 after hire purchase restrictions were lifted, and might return to this level if reductions in purchase tax coincided with the availability of a medium-priced colour set, although this is unlikely to be the case until after 1970. Cuts in purchase tax would however stimulate replacement demand.

The rate of growth of expenditure on the larger electrical domestic appliances is not expected to regain the high levels prevailing in the 1950's, even if total consumers' expenditure rises more rapidly than expected in the 1960's. Home sales of washing machines and refrigerators were in the region of £93 million in 1961; they reached a peak of about £120 million in 1959, and would also respond to changes in purchase tax. This is less true of expenditure on furniture and furnishings, which are only subject to purchase tax of 10 per cent. The largest annual increase in sales in the furnishing sector so far has been £37 million (at constant 1958 prices) in 1959.

More accurate estimates of how an increase in consumers' expenditure would be distributed between the different sectors of demand can be made on the basis of expenditure and price elasticities, where these are available. Table 74 shows the increased expenditure which might have resulted in certain sectors from an increase of, for example, 2·9 per cent in total consumers' expenditure in 1961. This assumes that prices remain constant and that the whole increase in expenditure is derived from a direct increase in consumers' disposable income.

TABLE 74 *The Effects on Certain Sectors of Demand of a Hypothetical Rise of 2·9 per cent in Total Consumers' Expenditure in 1961*

Actual expenditure in 1961 [£ million]	Estimated expenditure elasticity[1]	Change by sector in volume of expenditure after total rise of 2·9 per cent in all consumer spending %	£ million	
4,989	0·6	1·7	86·8	Food
1,051	0·7	2·0	21·3	Alcoholic drink
1,218	0·8	2·3	28·3	Tobacco
1,599	0·6	1·7	27·8	Housing
793	1·2	3·5	27·6	Fuel and light
1,388	1·4	4·1	56·4	Clothing
299	1·0	2·9	8·7	Footwear
386	2·0	5·8	22·4	Furniture and floor coverings

[1] Source: C. T. Saunders 'A Ten Year Projection for the British Economy' in 'Europe's Future in Figures', ed. Geary. Amsterdam 1962.

TABLE 75 *The Effects on Certain Sectors of Demand of Hypothetical Changes in Purchase Tax in 1961*

Actual expenditure in 1961 [£million]	Estimated price[3] elasticity	Change in purchase tax		Estimated reduction in price	Change in volume of expenditure after cut in purchase tax		
		From[1] [%]	To [%]	[%]	[%]	[£million]	
1,388	—0·3	5	0	3·6	1·1	15·3	Clothing
299	—0·3	5	0	3·6	1·1	3·3	Footwear
386	—0·6	5	0	3·6	2·2	8·5	Furniture and floor coverings
93	—1 to —2	25	20	3·2	3·2–6·4	3·0–5·9	Washing machines and refrigerators[2]
75	—1 to —2	50	30	11·0	11·0–22·0	8·25–16·5	Radio and television sets

[1] These were the rates prevailing from March 1961.
[2] Price elasticity for these goods might be expected to be higher than for radio and television, since ownership levels are further from saturation.
[3] Source: for clothing, footwear and furniture, C. T. Saunders (see Table 74); for electrical appliances, National Institute Economic Review, November 1960— 'The Demand for Domestic Appliances'.

Table 75 shows the increase in expenditure which might be expected to follow reductions in purchase tax on certain articles, considered separately from any direct increase in consumers' income.

The elasticities used as a basis for these calculations are all estimates, but some have a greater degree of reliability than others. The expenditure elasticity for housing, and the expenditure and price elasticities for furniture, must, in particular, be treated with caution. Elasticities are less useful in estimating changes in expenditure on durable consumer goods, since demand for these is influenced by a number of special factors, such as ownership levels and hire purchase restrictions, and are correspondingly more difficult to calculate. Price elasticities for the major electrical consumer durable goods are believed to be between −1 and −2,[1] and calculations for radio and television sets, washing machines and refrigerators have been included in Table 75 on this assumption, although they could well be invalidated by other market factors. The estimate for television sets in particular is likely to be affected by the fact that the greater part of sales is now made to rental companies rather than directly to the consumer. In the case of motor vehicles it is felt that too large a number of other factors are involved for an elasticity calculation[2] to be useful.

In practice the additional income would be likely to be distributed to consumers both directly and through purchase tax relief, and this would tend to give double benefit to durable consumer goods. It may be assumed that the motor industry, together with the radio and television, electrical domestic appliance and furniture industries, are those likely to derive the largest percentage increases in demand from a total increase in all consumers' expenditure. The food processing and clothing industries, on the other hand, would be likely to receive the largest quantitative increases.

There is a third possibility facing consumers when their total disposable income is increased, and this is to work shorter hours rather than to spend or save their extra money. It was estimated at the beginning of 1961[3] that out of 13 million wage earners some 60 per cent had a normal working week (exclusive of overtime) of 42 hours or less, while

---

[1] National Institute Economic Review, November 1960: 'The Demand for Domestic Appliances'.

[2] The figure most often quoted is an income elasticity of 2·4. This would give an increase on 1961 spending on cars of £34 million, assuming that there was no change in purchase tax.

[3] Clegg. Implications of the Shorter Working Week for Management. British Institute of Management 1962.

29 per cent still had a working week of 44 hours or more. In recent years there has been a very gradual trend towards shorter total working hours, which have fallen for men aged over 21 in manufacturing industry from an average 48·2 hours a week (including overtime) in October, 1959 to an average 46·8 hours in October, 1961. A 40-hour week is one of the current aims of the Trade Union Congress.

TABLE 76 *Average Weekly Earnings and Hours Worked, 1955–1961*

Men aged over 21 in manufacturing industry

Average weekly earnings (constant prices[1])		Annual change	Average weekly hours	Annual change	
s.	d.	%		%	
231	1		48·7		1955
234	1	+1·3	48·2	−1·0	1956
242	6	+3·6	48·0	−0·4	1957
239	9	−1·1	47·3	−1·5	1958
254	1	+6·0	48·2	+1·9	1959
		+2·2		−0·4	Average annual change[3]
284	3		48·2		1959[2]
300	3	+5·6	47·4	−1·7	1960
304	2	+1·3	46·8	−1·3	1961
		+3·4		−1·5	Average annual change[3]

[1] Base years 1955 and 1959.
[2] New series.
[3] Cumulative annual rate based on a least squares regression line.
Source: Ministry of Labour.

It is difficult to relate reductions in working hours to increases in earnings, since the total of hours worked depends on the amount of overtime offered by employers, as well as on the individual worker's decision as to whether to accept overtime work or not, and it can be argued that the fall in hours in recent years is entirely due to a decline in economic activity. There is also some doubt as to whether the current trend will continue. Owing to the fact that the American statistics of weekly hours worked include men, women and part-time workers in one total, it is often stated that the American worker works an appreciably shorter week than his British counterpart, and consequently that higher average wages would lead to a substantial reduction in British working hours. A recent survey[1] has however shown, by extracting part-time workers from the official average, that the American full-time worker in fact works for between 46 and 47 hours a week (including overtime). Comparable figures for this country are 47·4 hours for men and 39·7 hours for women, and it may be concluded from this that the British worker is likely to continue to work at the existing level.

Experience over recent years in any case suggests that an increase in consumer disposable income of 2·6 per cent is not on a large enough scale to have any appreciable effect on working hours, although of course in normal circumstances a large proportion of an increase in disposable income may be attributed to working overtime.

METHODS OF DISTRIBUTING ADDITIONAL INCOME TO CONSUMERS

1. *Income tax relief.* It was pointed out in the previous section that measures of income tax relief are an uncertain method of stimulating consumers' expenditure, since a proportion of the increase in disposable incomes is likely to be saved. Tax reliefs would however be a popular item in any government plan for adjustment to a purely civil economy, and provided that more is given away in reduced taxes than it has been decided to draw from consumers in the form of increased expenditure, they would constitute one method of replacing the defence expenditure which ceased with disarmament.

It is therefore interesting to see the cost of various measures of income tax relief. Income tax paid to the exchequer in the financial year 1960–1961 amounted to £2,433 million. Approximately half of income tax revenue is normally derived from tax paid on wages, salaries, forces' pay, family allowances and certain pensions. The rest is paid on dividends, interest and trading incomes. The standard rate of income tax has been 7s. 9d in the pound since March, 1959. This is paid both by private persons and by companies, but the tax is graduated for the individual taxpayer by means of personal allowances and reliefs and reduced rates of tax, whereas companies receive no allowances and reliefs of this type and are liable at the standard rate on their whole income.

[1] De Grazia. 'Of Time, Work and Leisure' Twentieth Century Fund 1962.

It has been estimated that the yield of each penny of the standard rate of income tax is currently £25 million, which rises to £30 million if the reduced rates of tax are included. A concession of £500 million could therefore lower the standard rate to 6s. 5d, and the reduced rates similarly by 1s. 4d each, while a concession of £710 million given with a view to increasing expenditure by £500 million could lower the rates by 2s. each. A large proportion of this relief would however go to companies rather than to consumers. Among consumers the highest income groups would derive the most benefit, and this factor would make it more likely that the addition to income would be saved rather than spent.

In order to give income tax relief to consumers rather than to companies, therefore, concessions would have to be made on personal allowances and reliefs rather than on the standard rate charged. The cost of making changes in allowances varies from year to year; on the basis of the 1961 figures, however, it has been estimated that the cost of raising the earned income allowance from $\frac{2}{9}$ to $\frac{1}{4}$ would be in the region of £100 million. This concession would not affect retired people, and an increase in personal allowances may be felt to be more equitable; the cost of increasing the personal allowance for a single person from £140 to £160, and for a married man from £240 to £260, has been estimated at some £120 million. Further concessions to families with dependent children would be a means of ensuring that a higher proportion of the additional income was spent; the cost of increasing all the children's allowances, which currently range from £100 to £150, by £20, is estimated at just under £40 million. To the same end income tax on family allowances and small private pensions could be abolished; revenue from this source amounted to £16 million in 1960.

2. *Purchase tax relief.* An increase in consumers' disposable income brought about by purchase tax relief gives the government considerably more control over consumers' expenditure than is the case with income tax relief. The great majority of goods on which purchase tax is paid are consumer goods, so that nearly the whole of any cut in revenue would go to benefit consumers. The possibility that a proportion of the conceded revenue will be saved rather than spent is considerably reduced, as reductions in purchase tax on the more expensive consumer goods tend to bring new customers for them into the market, rather than make consumers who would have bought them in any case feel that their incomes have been increased. The government can also maintain control over the pattern of consumer spending, by discriminatory tax cuts.

M 2

Purchase tax is levied on the majority of durable consumer goods, and also on clothing, stationery, drugs, perfumery and cosmetics. It is an *ad valorem* tax expressed as a percentage of the wholesale value of the goods concerned. Estimated receipts from purchase tax in 1960–1961 amounted to £511·1 million. Receipts from certain main commodities were as follows:

TABLE 77 *Approximate Yield from Purchase Tax, 1960–1961*

Rate of tax [per cent]	Approximate yield [£ million]	Commodity
5	51·2	Clothing and footwear
12·5	16·4	Floor coverings
5	9·4	Furniture
25	33·3	Domestic gas, electric and other appliances
50	41·3	Radio and television sets, and valves
50	11·1	Gramophones, radiograms and records
50	172·2	Motor cars
25	8·0	Motor cycles
50	28·4	Perfumery and cosmetics
25	10·4	Drugs and medicines
5–25	129·4	Other
	511·1	Total

Source: Customs and Excise Commissioners: 52nd Report, 1961.

Rates of purchase tax were changed on several articles in 1961, and total receipts in 1961–1962 amounted to just over £520 million. Purchase tax on radio and television sets, cars and cosmetics now stands at 45 per cent, while clothing, floor coverings and furniture are charged at 10 per cent. Estimated receipts for 1962–1963, however, show little change at £535 million.

The complete abolition of purchase tax could therefore be achieved by the diversion to the exchequer of little more than £500 million from the defence budget. Although a high proportion of this sum would be spent, there would be a certain element of saving involved, and it would also be unlikely that a government would wish to deprive itself entirely of this source of revenue, or of this means of control over the economy. It is probable however that various purchase tax reductions would be made in order to encourage demand for the products of certain industries. An obvious choice would be the motor industry; on the basis of the

1960–1961 figures, the cost of reducing purchase tax on motor cars to 25 per cent[1] would have been in the region of £86 million. Similarly for the electronics industry, purchase tax on radios, television sets, gramophones and records could have been reduced to 25 per cent at the cost of some £26 million. There is wide scope for further reductions to benefit the domestic electrical appliance industry and clothing and furniture manufacturers.

3. *The Social Services.* Income could also be redistributed to specific groups of consumers through increased social service payments, rather than to consumers in general through tax reliefs. This form of increasing consumers' disposable incomes would be more likely to generate the full amount of replacement demand for goods and services, as it would be unlikely that old age pensioners and widows, people drawing unemployment or sickness benefit or people living on national assistance would save any increase in their incomes, and it would be probable that any increase in family allowances would also largely be spent.

The pattern of expenditure of any increase in social service payments

TABLE 78 *Distribution of Household Expenditure in Various Categories of Households*

1953-54 consumption valued at January 1956 prices
Percentage of Total Expenditure

Single pensioners	Pensioner couples	Widowed mothers	Index[1] households	
18·0	12·4	13·2	8·7	Housing
14·6	10·3	9·5	5·5	Fuel, light and power
38·8	40·7	50·6	35·0	Food
4·8	6·8	7·0	10·6	Clothing and footwear
3·1	3·7	2·3	6·6	Durable household goods
5·1	5·5	5·9	5·9	Other goods
2·0	2·3	3·5	6·8	Transport
5·8	4·0	5·4	5·8	Services
2·8	6·1	0·1	7·1	Alcoholic drink
5·0	8·2	2·5	8·0	Tobacco
100·0	100·0	100·0	100·0	

[1] This reduction was in fact made in November, 1962.
[2] The average households used as a basis for the Ministry of Labour retail price index.
Source: T. Lynes, National Assistance and National Prosperity. Occasional Papers on Social Administration. January, 1962.

would however be unlikely to resemble that of a sum distributed to consumers in general through tax reliefs. The greater part of any increase would certainly be spent on non-durable goods, and probably also on housing. In 1960 old age pensioner households spent on average 27s. 10d per head per week on food, as compared to an average for all households of 29s. 8d; old age pensioners spent slightly more than the average on bread, tea and fats and appreciably less on meat, fruit and vegetables, and on all convenience foods. As a proportion of total income, however, pensioners and other households in the lowest income groups spend more on food, as well as on fuel and housing, than the average household. Table 78 shows the distribution of household expenditure in some of these income groups in 1953–54.

Since rising prices have invalidated much of the improvement made in social security payments since 1953/54, it seems probable that the pattern of expenditure in pensioner and similar households has shown little change. Additional income would probably result in even greater proportionate spending on food, fuel and housing, and also in a sharp increase in spending on clothing.

Increases in social security payments would be felt by many people to have a clear priority if defence expenditure were to be redistributed, and they would also constitute a reliable method of stimulating replacement demand. Examples are given in the rest of this section of the estimated costs of making increases in the various categories of social service payments.

National Insurance

National insurance benefits, and in particular old age pensions, would be likely to have the highest priority if money became available to increase current spending on the social services. At the end of 1961, 5·7 million people were drawing old age pensions, while 590,000 were drawing widows' allowances and guardians' benefits; over the year sickness benefit was being paid to an average of 930,000 a week and unemployment benefit to an average of 185,000. The flat-rate old age pension was raised in April, 1961 from 50s. to 57s. 6d for a single person and from 80s. to 92s. 6d for a married couple; only 200,000 people had qualified for additional graduated pensions (of 6d a week for each £7 10s. of graduated contributions paid by a man or for each £9 paid by a woman) by the end of 1961. Sickness, unemployment, maternity and widows' benefits are paid at similar rates, with increases for dependents.

The exchequer contribution to the national insurance fund amounted to £170 million in the financial year 1960–61; the 1961–62 payment is estimated at £187 million. The National Insurance Act of 1959, which introduced the graduated pension scheme, fixed the exchequer supplement at one-quarter of the national insurance contributions, (exclusive of graduated contributions[1]), paid by employers and employees, and at one-third of contributions paid by self-employed or non-employed persons.[2] The new scheme began to operate in April 1961, when flat-rate contributions and benefits were increased as well as the exchequer supplement, and graduated contributions began to be paid.

TABLE 79 *Receipts and Payments of the National Insurance Fund*

£million

1960–61	1961–62 estimate	Receipts	1960–61	1961–62 estimate	Payments
713·0	937·0	Contributions from employers and insured persons			Benefits:
			676·9	776·0	Retirement
			65·9	81·0	Widows' and guardians'
170·0	187·0	Exchequer supplements	30·2	44·0	Unemployment
			135·0	155·0	Sickness
			20·6	23·0	Maternity
15·3	50·0	Interest etc.	5·8	6·0	Death grant
			934·5	1,085·0	Total benefits
38·7	nil	Transfer from Reserve Fund	38·1	41·0	Administrative expenses
			4·8	8·0	Transfer to N. Ireland N.I.F.
			0·8	nil	Other
937·0	1,174·0		978·2	1,134·0	
41·2	nil	Excess of payments over receipts	nil	40·0	Excess of receipts over payments

[1] i.e. there is no exchequer contribution to graduated pensions.
[2] A provision was made for additional payments from the exchequer in 1960 61 and 1961–62.

The total cost of the changes in the national insurance scheme was estimated by the government actuary at £141 million for 1961–62, rising to £173 million by 1971–72. The share of retirement pensions in 1961–62 was estimated at £100 million; since the graduated pensions becoming payable in that year could only be at very low rates, almost the whole of this £100 million represents the cost of increasing the flat-rate old age pension.

It is difficult to estimate the cost of a future increase in the flat-rate retirement pension with any degree of accuracy, since on the one hand the numbers of men over 65 and women over 60 are increasing rapidly, and on the other the graduated pension scheme gives a strong incentive to those earning over £9 a week to delay retirement. According to the current government estimate, the total cost of flat-rate retirement pensions will increase from £776 million in 1961–62 to £994 million in 1971–72, or by 25 per cent, without allowing for any increase in the standard rate of pension, and the cost of the 1961 increases will have risen to £125 million by 1971–72. Another increase of 7s. 6d for a single person and 12s. 6d for a married couple, therefore, which cost some £100 million in 1961–62, would be likely to cost between £100 million and £125 million a year if it took place in the years between 1961–62 and 1971–72.

The number of claims for the other national insurance benefits normally remains relatively steady, although government estimates of the cost of future claims are based on the arbitrary assumption of an increased rate of unemployment, and the cost of widows' allowances is expected to start to fall just before 1970. If it is assumed that disarmament would not cause a significant increase in the unemployment rate, the cost of raising the standard rate of benefit for all claims other than retirement pensions by the same amounts as in 1961[1] can be estimated as likely to be in the region of £41 million. The government estimate of the cost of the 1961 increase by 1971–72, on the basis of a 3 per cent rate of unemployment, is £48 million.

If, therefore, some £170 million of defence expenditure were diverted to the national insurance fund, all flat-rate benefits could be increased by amounts similar to those granted in April 1961. This would represent an increase of over 90 per cent in the exchequer supplement to the

---

[1] i.e. by 7s. 6d. on the rate for a single adult, by 5s. on the rate for dependent adults, by 2s. 6d. for dependent children and by 12s. 6d. for widowed mothers. For fuller details see the Report of the Ministry of Pensions and National Insurance, 1961.

fund in 1961–62, and of over 85 and 80 per cent respectively in the exchequer supplements estimated for 1966–67 and 1971–72. This would imply that the basis for calculating the exchequer supplement be changed from 25 per cent of flat rate contributions by employers and employees to approximately 50 per cent.

National Assistance

The cost of national assistance is not covered by any insurance contributions, but is met entirely from the exchequer. Total expenditure by the National Assistance Board in 1961 amounted to £184·8 million, made up as follows:—

£ million

163·2	National assistance grants
9·2	Non-contributory old age pensions
0·4	Reception and re-establishment centres
12·0	Administrative expenses

184·8

The number of grants of weekly national assistance allowances being paid at the end of 1961 was 1,844,000, and the number of non-contributory old age pensions was 135,000. Over 57 per cent of national assistance weekly grants consisted of supplements to national insurance retirement pensions, and a further 14 per cent consisted of supplements to other national insurance benefits.

National assistance is paid according to a scale of requirements, altered periodically by the Minister of Pensions, which fixes the minimum sums on which it is believed that a single person or married couple can live, together with allowances for dependents. The scale is exclusive of rent or rates, for which separate allowances are made. The scale rates were last increased in September 1962, when they were raised from 53s. 6d to 57s. 6d for a single householder, and from 90s. to 95s. 6d for a married couple.[1] The national assistance scale is therefore similar to the flat-rate retirement pension for a single person, and 3s. higher than the flat-rate retirement pension for a married couple, and the National Assistance Board will pay in addition the rent or rates of pensioners with no other source of income. The national assistance scale is also similar to the unemployment or sickness benefit for a single

[1] For details of other rates for dependents and blind and tuberculous persons, see National Assistance Board, Explanatory Memorandum on Draft National Assistance Amendment Regulations 1962.

person, but national assistance grants for dependents are higher, and again rent or rates will be paid.

If a proportion of defence expenditure were used to increase flat-rate retirement pensions and other national insurance benefits on the scale suggested in the previous section, a large number of people now drawing national assistance would become ineligible for it or only eligible for smaller additional weekly payments. An increase in national insurance benefits without a corresponding increase in national assistance scale rates would mean that there was no net increase in spending power for over a million old age pensioners and other persons living on both national insurance and national assistance, who would simply pay a larger proportion of their rents from their pensions or other national insurance benefits and a smaller proportion from their national assistance supplements. If flat-rate retirement pensions were raised to 65s. for a single person and 105s. for a married couple, and other flat-rate national insurance benefits to 65s., national assistance scale rates would have to be brought up to 65s. for a single person and 108s. for a married couple, with the corresponding increases for dependents,[1] in order to allow the full increases in national insurance benefits to be enjoyed by the persons concerned.

This would involve no additional cost in national assistance to persons with national insurance benefits, who would continue to receive supplements of the same amount. The additional cost would be in the increased national assistance allowances to persons not drawing national insurance. National assistance weekly allowances were being paid to 532,000 persons in this category, and also to their dependents, in December, 1961. Since one effect of raising the scale rates tends to be to make more people eligible for national assistance, their numbers are likely to have increased in September, 1962 and would increase again if the scale rate rose to 65s. On the basis of the numbers in December, 1961, however, and of the scale rates for September, 1962, the extra cost of paying national assistance at the rates of 65s. to single and 108s. to married persons in this category, and of increasing their dependents' allowances by 2s. 6d, would be in the region of £13 million. This figure is not likely to be significantly altered by an increase in the numbers eligible.[2]

---

[1] by 2s. 6d. for each child under 16.

[2] The largest increase in the total number of national assistance weekly allowances following a rise in the scale rate in recent years was after that in September, 1959. Allowances rose then by some 60,000 more than the usual amount between August and October, but that rise was not accompanied by an increase in national insurance benefits.

According to a recent survey,[1] an increase of this size would be almost sufficient, assuming that there had been no rise in the price index for low income households after September, 1959, to restore national assistance scale rates to the same position as they held in July, 1948 in relation to the general level of real incomes.

Family Allowances

Family allowances, like national assistance benefits, are paid entirely from the exchequer, at a cost in 1961 of over £133·5 million. This showed an increase of 2·6 per cent on the previous year, representing the increase in the number of children in families receiving allowances. The rate of allowance itself has not been changed since October, 1956.

The current allowances are 8s. a week for the second child in the family and 10s. a week for the third and each subsequent child, with an upper age limit of 15, except for children who stay on at school. No allowance is payable for the eldest child. Over 60 per cent of families receiving allowances have two children only, and are consequently in receipt of only one allowance.

At 31st January, 1961, second child's allowances were being paid on behalf of 3,569,000 children and third and subsequent child's allowances were being paid on behalf of 2,196,000 children. The cost of raising the second child's allowance from 8s. to 10s. would therefore at that point have been £18·6 million a year, and the cost of raising the 10s. allowance to 12s. 6d would have been £14·3 million, making a total of £32·9 million. Since the child population increased during 1961 by 2·6 per cent, the cost at the beginning of 1962 would have been just over £33·5 million.

[1] T. Lynes. National Assistance and National Prosperity. Occasional Papers on Social Administration. January, 1962.

Chapter 15

The Redistribution of Defence Expenditure through Government Current Expenditure at Home and Increased Aid Abroad

In the event of disarmament there would be a wide scope for the replacement of defence expenditure by increases in other forms of government current expenditure on goods and services. This method of replacing defence expenditure could be very rapidly carried out, and it would also have the merit of being easily controlled. Among several possibilities the most obvious would be to transfer defence expenditure to the wages and salaries of government employees. This would give a further stimulus to consumer expenditure; as a method of replacing demand, however, it is subject to the same qualification as an increase in consumers' incomes through tax relief, which is that more must be given away than it is intended should be spent, in order to cover the saving of a proportion of the increase. It is also subject to a further qualification, which is that a proportion of the increase in wages and salaries will be returned to the exchequer as tax, so that this also must be allowed for in calculating the additional demand.

The other main item of government expenditure which it seems most suitable to increase in place of defence expenditure is aid to developing countries. The costs of these two possibilities are discussed in the rest of this chapter.

INCREASES IN WAGES AND SALARIES OF GOVERNMENT EMPLOYEES

Many government employees are paid less than those in comparable employment in private organisations. This is particularly true of the professional grades, and there would be a strong case for decreasing the differentials between salaries in these sectors and those of other professional workers if a large sum of money became available to the exchequer for redistribution. The most publicised examples have been those of teachers and nurses, and these cases are examined more closely in this section. Money could also be well spent, however, on increasing the salaries of other types of government employee, or employees whose salaries are partly paid by the exchequer, including probation officers, university lecturers, local government officials and several others.

Teachers. The education service is financed partly by the exchequer and partly by the local education authorities out of local rates. Teachers in state schools are paid by the local authority, but an appreciable proportion of their salaries is provided by the exchequer, and the salary scales negotiated by the Burnham Committee must be approved by the Minister of Education. The total cost of salaries paid to teachers in primary and secondary schools in 1960–61 was £264·5 million, the number of teachers at the end of the financial year being just over 269,000.

In 1961 the salary claim put forward by the Burnham Committee was for an average increase of 16·25 per cent, which would have raised the basic salary scale for the non-graduate 3-year trained teacher[1] from £520 to £1,000 (after 16 years' service) to £600 to £1,200. The cost of this increase was estimated at £47·5 million. The government offer, which the teachers finally accepted, was an increase of 14·6 per cent at a cost of £42 million, giving a basic scale of £570 to £1,170.

The salary increase advocated by the National Union of Teachers in 1961 was for an average of 25 per cent, giving a basic scale of £700 to £1,300 after 10 years' service. The cost of this claim was then estimated at £100 million. In 1962 the N.U.T. objective was raised to a basic scale of £775 to £1,375.

A new Burnham agreement will be negotiated during the financial year 1962–63 to come into force in April 1963, and it seems certain that the teachers will then be given more than the £5·5 million which was deducted from their claim in 1961. The cost of implementing the N.U.T.'s proposal for 1961 will as a result fall to an amount slightly in excess of £50 million.[2] The diversion of defence funds to teachers' salaries could well be carried out on this scale, and many people would feel that an even larger one would be justified.

Nurses. Over 70 per cent of the cost of the National Health Service is financed by the exchequer, the rest being met largely by National

[1] From 1963 all new teachers will have had 3 years' training.
[2] These calculations assume no significant change in the number of teachers, but the cost will begin to increase after 1965 when the rate of recruitment is expected to rise.

Health Service contributions and from local rates. The pay claim put forward in August, 1961 on behalf of the total of approximately 200,000 nurses and midwives employed in the hospital services was for an average increase of from 25 to 30 per cent. This would have brought a staff nurse, after three years' training and six years' experience, from the present maximum of £656 a year on to a scale ranging from £650 to £850[1] a year, and a sister from a maximum of £840 to a scale ranging from £900 to £1,150. The total cost was estimated at between £40 and £50 million.

The government offer in reply to the 1961 claim, which has not been accepted at the date of writing, was an increase of 2·5 per cent, at a cost of £3·3 million, in 1962. A further £6·6 million was offered over the next two years. If this offer turns out to be final, therefore, the additional £30 to £40 million necessary to meet the 1961 claim might be found from defence expenditure.

INCREASES IN AID TO DEVELOPING COUNTRIES

1. Total Aid to Developing Countries, 1956–1961. It was estimated in a United Nations report[2] of 1951 that, in order to increase national income per head in all the underdeveloped countries by 2 per cent a year, the annual capital import by these countries should exceed £3,000 million. At current prices this figure would be in the region of £3,600 million. In practice, however, the annual flow of official and private funds to the developing countries from Organisation for European Economic Cooperation member countries and associates (including the United States) averaged some £2,400 million[3] between 1956 and 1959, and reached £2,762 million and £3,100 million in 1960 and 1961. The average annual contribution from Australia, New Zealand and Japan between 1956 and 1959 was £107 million, and the average annual contribution from the U.S.S.R. and other communist

---

[1] All the rates are subject to deductions for maintenance.

[2] 'Measures for the Economic Development of Underdeveloped Countries'. U.N. 1951. Mainland China has been excluded from the underdeveloped countries considered here and throughout this section.

[3] Excluding military aid and I.M.F. movements. This estimate is taken from 'The Flow of Financial Resources to Countries in Course of Economic Development' '1956–1959' and '1960' (O.E.E.C. 1961 and 1962). The U.N. estimate (see note 1, p. 175) is lower at £1,786 million, since it excludes grants for current purposes from France and other W. European countries to overseas territories, French gross private investment in the franc area, export credit guarantees and other short-term capital flows.

countries between 1954 and 1960 was £163 million.[1] The average rate of growth of income per head in the developing countries during the 1950's was 1 per cent.[2]

Just under 40 per cent of the total capital provided by what are now member countries of the Organisation for Economic Cooperation and Development came from private sources, while the rest consisted of grants and loans from governments and international organisations. The greater part of aid was bilateral, only 8 per cent being given as contributions to multilateral agencies. Over half of total aid was provided by the United States, some two-thirds of which came from the U.S. government. France was the second largest contributor, although the official total of French aid includes the cost of administering French overseas territories, which may amount to some 20 per cent. Even

TABLE 80 *Public and Private Aid to Developing Countries in 1960 in Relation to Gross National Product*

O.E.C.D. countries and Japan

Total contributions [£million]	Contributions as a percentage of g.n.p.	Donor Country
1,350	0·78	United States
460	2·22	France[1]
306	1·32	United Kingdom[2]
220	0·93	West Germany
106	0·93	Italy
91	0·66	Japan
88	2·18	Netherlands
64	1·54	Belgium
53	1·81	Switzerland
48	0·36	Canada
2,853		Total, including other O.E.C.D. countries

[1] Including administrative expenditure in overseas territories.
[2] Including oil companies' investment abroad.
Source: 'The Flow of Financial Resources to Countries in Course of Economic Development' and O.E.E.C. General Statistics.

[1] 'International Flow of Long-term Capital and Official Donations, 1951–59, U.N. 1961. Aid from the communist countries does not include aid from them to communist underdeveloped countries.
[2] 'Capital Development Needs of the Less Developed Countries' U.N. 1962.

without this proportion, French aid would still have exceeded British aid by some £479 million between 1956 and 1959. If aid is measured as a proportion of gross national product, however, the French, Dutch, Swiss and Belgian contributions are all larger than those of the United States and the United Kingdom.

The distribution of both public and private aid has been uneven, a large proportion of public aid having tended to go to countries subject to communist pressure, and more than one-third of private investment having gone to the oil producing countries. The countries receiving the largest amount of public aid per head between 1957 and 1959 were Jordan, Libya, Israel, South Korea and the Lebanon, while the largest concentration of private investment was in Latin America, the Middle East and North Africa. There has been no tendency for the countries with the lowest amount of national income per head to receive more aid than those in a more advanced stage of development.

2. *The Structure of British Aid to Developing Countries, 1956–61.* The structure of British aid to developing countries between 1956 and 1959 differed from the structure of American aid in that two-thirds of the total consisted of private investment. The bulk of this was in the form of direct investment, and investment by U.K. oil companies made up a large proportion. Since 1959, however, there has been a sharp rise in government aid; total government grants and loans to developing countries in the financial year 1961/62 is expected to amount to £180 million, which will represent an increase of over 100 per cent on the figure for 1957/58. Private investment, on the other hand, has been falling since 1959 and total British aid has in fact shown a slight decline.

TABLE 81 *The Flow of British Capital to Developing Countries, 1955–1961*

£million 1956–1959[1] Total	1960[2]	1961[2]	
			Government assistance:
320	125	155	bilateral[3]
79	25	7	multilateral
726	154	138	Private investment (net of disinvestment)
1,125	304	300	Total

[1] Source: O.E.E.C.
[2] Source: Treasury, Central Statistical Office.
[3] The figures do not cover all technical assistance, some of which cannot be quantitatively assessed.

In 1961 just over 60 per cent of total bilateral aid provided by the British government went to colonial territories, and just over 32 per cent to independent Commonwealth countries. The main sources through which aid is channelled are as follows:—

Bilateral aid

Organisation	Areas covered	Financial scale
The Colonial Development Corporation	Known as the Commonwealth Development Corporation since August 1962. Its work will in future be extended to Commonwealth countries.	A total of up to £160 million can be lent at any one time, of which £130 million is obtainable from the exchequer. Outstanding loans at the end of 1961 were £115 million; new loans during 1961 were £10 million.
The Colonial Development and Welfare Fund	Provides grants as well as loans.	Funds voted for 1959–1964 are £140·5 million, of which £33 million remains to be allocated. New grants and loans in 1961/62 amounted to £26 million.
Exchequer loans	Made to colonial territories.	Up to £100 million from 1959 to 1964, with a limit of £25 million in any one year. New loans in 1961/62 were £19 million, bringing the total to £50 million.
Export Credits Guarantee Department	Grants economic assistance loans to Commonwealth and other countries. These must be spent on the purchase of British and preferably capital goods.	Loans to Commonwealth countries in 1960/61 were £37·5 million and loans to other countries £2 million.

*Bilateral and
multilateral aid*

Organisation	Areas covered	Financial scale
Department of Technical Co-operation	Set up in June, 1961. Supplies technical assistance to Commonwealth, colonial and foreign countries, both directly and through international organisations.	Budget for 1962/63, £28·4 million.

Other government bilateral aid is given under the Foreign Office Grants and Services Vote, the Commonwealth Services Vote and the Colonial Services Vote. Bilateral aid from these sources amounted to some £39 million in 1960/61. Multilateral aid is also provided through the Foreign Office Vote, under which grants are made to United Nations organisations, and through the Commonwealth Services Vote, as to the Indus Basin Development Fund. Multilateral aid from these sources amounted to some £6 million in 1960/61. The greater part of multilateral aid is however provided through the U.K. subscriptions to the International Bank for Reconstruction and Development and to the International Development Association, which amounted to nearly £15 million in 1960/61.

3. Aid in the 1960's and the Transfer of Resources released by Disarmament.
In the event of disarmament the extent to which funds could usefully be transferred from defence expenditure to developing countries would be limited by the capacity of these countries to absorb foreign capital efficiently. This is determined both by the degree to which pre-investment planning has been carried out and by the quality of the administrative machinery available, and although these factors are difficult to measure it is clear that present need greatly exceeds the present flow of capital, and that future needs will be larger still. Within the donor countries, however, other limits would be set to this redistribution of resources by the necessity to use defence funds to maintain employment at home, and also by balance of payments considerations.

A recent survey[1] has estimated that in order to achieve the 1951 aim

[1] Paul G. Hoffman 'One Hundred Countries, One and One Quarter Billion People'. Lasker Foundation. Washington D.C. 1960. This assumes a capital output ratio of 3 to 1.

of increasing the annual rate of growth of income per head in the developing countries to 2 per cent, an additional £1,070 million of development capital would now be needed from the developed countries in each year of the 1960's. This represents an increase of 60 per cent on the average annual total flow of aid, according to the U.N. figures, from both multilateral and bilateral sources between 1956 and 1959. Total annual aid as measured by the O.E.C.D. increased by some 30 per cent, or by £700 million, between 1959 and 1961, but in 1959 approximately one-third of this total did not consist of development capital according to the U.N. classification. Since, however, the main increase in aid over the last two years has been from government sources, and the greater part of government aid normally falls within the U.N. definition, it seems likely that at least £500 million of the necessary additional capital is already being provided. The United States has announced plans to increase official aid by a further 50 per cent between 1961 and 1964, and other O.E.C.D. members, not including the United Kingdom or France, have also planned substantial increases, so that it seems probable that this target will be reached in the mid-1960's.

A minimum use of the resources released by disarmament would be to make good any deficiencies remaining in this level of contributions, and to add a further £1,070 million of development capital, bringing the rate of growth of income per head in the underdeveloped countries to 3 per cent.[1] A more generous use of defence expenditure would be to add a further £2,140 million of development capital, and attempt to raise the rate of growth of income per head to 4 per cent. The smaller of these two programmes would involve a total increase in contributions by O.E.C.D. members of over 50 per cent on the total for 1961, of which nearly one-third is likely to be achieved in any case by 1964. This increase would bring total contributions from O.E.C.D. members to over 1 per cent of their aggregate national products. The larger programme would involve a total increase in contributions of 85 per cent on 1961, of which under one-quarter would be achieved in any case by 1964.

The cost of increasing British aid to underdeveloped countries from 50 per cent to 85 per cent on the total for 1961 would be between £150 million and £255 million. At present just over half of British aid is provided from governmental sources, but increases of this size in spending by the exchequer would bring the government's share to 70 per cent unless, as is likely, private investment in developing countries

[1] Assuming an annual rate of population growth of 2 per cent.

were stimulated by the rise in the total flow of financial resources to these countries.

4. Methods of Distributing Aid and their Effects on the Balance of Payments. The need for increasing the share of grants and 'soft' loans in total aid to developing countries has often been emphasised in recent years, as the rising cost of servicing foreign debt tends to cancel out an increasing proportion of the aid received by many developing countries. Balance of payments considerations, however, act as a disincentive to donor countries to increase the proportion of bilateral aid given on this basis, or to raise their contributions to the international organisations which operate in this way, although a general tendency towards easier forms of lending was recorded in 1961. Nearly 50 per cent of bilateral assistance given by the British government in 1961 was in the form of grants, and the terms of loans, which are made at market rates of interest, were eased through the extension of grace and maturity periods.

The United Kingdom balance of payments has fluctuated sharply in recent years. The balance on current account showed a marked

TABLE 82 *The United Kingdom Balance of Payments, 1959–1961, Military Expenditure Abroad and Aid to Developing Countries*

£million

1959	1960	1961	
—104	—391	—135	Visible balance
+219	+103	+65	Invisible balance
+115	—288	—70	Current balance
—499	—202	+8	Balance of long-term capital
—384	—490	—62	Balance of current and long-term capital
—21	+306	+81	Balancing item
+405	+184	—19	Balance of monetary movements
—130	—163	—187	Balance of military expenditure abroad
			U.K. government assistance for overseas development:
—55	—65	—79	Grants (affecting current balance)
n.a.	—84	—83	Loans (affecting balance of long-term capital)

Source: Cmnd. 1671. United Kingdom Balance of Payments, 1959–1961.

improvement in 1961, as a result of a downward trend in imports and an increase in exports, although military expenditure abroad increased and so did grants to developing countries. The long-term capital account also improved, but largely as a result of exceptional loan repayments from Europe and American investment.

On the basis of the 1961 figures, disarmament could improve the balance of payments on current account by at least £187 million, since the import content of expenditure on defence goods and services is not known. It can be assumed, however, that the increased expenditure by consumers and on domestic investment which would replace defence expenditure would have an appreciable import content, although its long-term effect could be to increase exports. It can also be assumed that virtually the whole of the British contribution to a United Nations force would be a debit item in the balance of payments; at the notional figure of 5 per cent of defence expenditure in 1961/62[1], this would amount to some £83 million. The net saving according to the figures that are available could therefore be in the region of £104 million. This would exceed current grants for overseas development by the U.K. government by £25 million, and should enable them to be more than doubled without significantly affecting the present balance of payments position.

The remainder of the increase in government aid would, however, constitute a debit item in the balance of payments, unless it were given in the form of tied loans, in which case it would in effect consist of a transfer payment within the domestic economy. Although tied loans are unlikely to lead to the most efficient distribution of a fixed amount of aid to developing countries, they may when balance of payments considerations are involved result in a larger total volume of aid than would otherwise have been given. There would be a strong case for combining expenditure on aid with expenditure to assist the reorganisation of the domestic industries affected by disarmament, and manufacturers in the electronics and aircraft industries in particular suggested in the course of interviews that suitable government action in the event of disarmament would be to finance purchases of their products by the developing countries. Communications equipment, heavy engineering products and all types of vehicles are needed by these countries, although in most cases not until the infrastructure of the economy has been sufficiently built up. Provided that untied grants for development are also sharply increased, an appreciable proportion of

[1] See the preface.

the additional aid could consist of bilateral loans tied to the purchase of goods from Britain. It would be of more direct use to British industry to tie the aid to the purchase of specific goods, but unless this is administered under a general and detailed plan, this type of aid can be of little use to the developing countries concerned. The existing form of tied aid, loans by the Export Credits Guarantee Department for goods sold to the developing countries, could also be considerably enlarged. On a smaller scale, aid might be given in the form of technical assistance from qualified and skilled workers made redundant by contractions in British industries; a proportion of the salaries of technicians working abroad would probably be remitted to the United Kingdom, but in any case this would not constitute a large debit item.

There is considerable precedent for giving aid in a tied form, although it is not a method which has normally been employed by the British Government, except in the work of the Export Credits Guarantee Department. Contributions from the United States Development Loan Fund[1] have been primarily made for the purchase of American goods and services since 1959, while loans from the American Export-Import Bank are wholly tied to American goods, and the International Co-operation Administration[1] makes gifts of agricultural commodities of which the U.S. has a surplus, although it procures other goods on a world-wide basis. Grants made by the French and West German governments have also frequently been tied.

A very high proportion of British bilateral aid would certainly continue to go to the colonial territories and independent Commonwealth countries, but unless restrictions were placed upon the spending of the money given or lent there would be no guarantee of its remaining within the sterling area. Developing countries and relatively poor countries which currently benefit from British military expenditure abroad would have a prior claim on aid to replace this source of support to their economies; these are all within the sterling area and include Libya, Gibraltar, Malta and Cyprus in the Mediterranean and Near East, Aden in the Middle East, Malaya and Singapore and Hong Kong in the Far East, and Kenya and the West Indies. Net military expenditure in the sterling area in 1961 amounted to £129 million; the proportion of this spent in developing countries cannot be estimated, but expenditure in Australia was probably large.

After compensatory assistance to these countries increased aid to

---

[1] Taken over by the Agency for International Development in 1961. In practice almost all A.I.D. operations are tied.

India might well be considered a major priority for the United Kingdom. The Indian Third Five-Year Plan, which covers the years from 1961–1966, aims at increasing income per head by 3 per cent in each of these years. The net investment required is estimated at £7,857 million of which £1,964 million, or an average £393 million a year, must be provided from external assistance. Aid to India is currently running well below the planned level; contributions pledged for 1962/63 amount to £310 million, leaving a gap of some £30 million between this amount and the total requested for the year. The British contribution was £30 million, which was appreciably smaller than the West German contribution of nearly £50 million. Since the U.S. has agreed to match total contributions by other countries, the British contribution would only have to have been increased to £45 million for the aid gap to be closed. This situation is likely to recur in subsequent years, and if as a result the targets of the Third Plan have to be cut as the targets of the Second Plan were, the social and political consequences to India could be very severe.

An increase in grants and 'soft' loans to organisations providing multilateral aid would also be desirable, since the first contributions to be increased should logically be to those concerned with pre-investment programmes and basic development. Outstanding examples are the U.N. Special Fund, which helps to finance development surveys and the creation of research and training facilities, and the Expanded Programme of Technical Assistance. These are still operating on a very small scale, the total value of pledges made to the Special Fund for 1962 being estimated at £20 million, and the cost of the E.P.T.A. programme for 1961 and 1962 being planned at just over £25 million. Total British grants to the Special Fund and E.P.T.A. for 1962 amount to under £3 million, and this is the second largest contribution. A general increase in subscriptions to the International Development Association, which provides interest free loans and tends to specialise in the basic projects of road and harbour construction, drainage and water supply, should also have priority. The freely usable portion of I.D.A.'s capital, which will become available between 1960 and 1964, amounts to £270 million, of which the U.K. will subscribe just under £47 million.

Whatever the immediate consequences to the balance of payments of a large increase in aid to the developing countries, the long term effects should prove favourable, as the result is likely to be to create new potential markets for British exports. The fact that all donor countries would be likely to increase their overseas aid at the same time would also tend to result in the immediate creation of new export prospects, as unless all new aid were tied to the goods of the donor country or British goods had become much more uncompetitive than is currently the case, a proportion of the resulting purchases by the developing countries would be likely to be made in the United Kingdom.

The balance of payments effects of disarmament would be uncertain for some time for all disarming countries. If these countries reacted to this uncertainty by restricting their imports and capital exports, a world economic crisis could follow, whereas a general increase in contributions to the developing countries as well as in domestic investment and consumers' expenditure could lead to a considerable stimulation of world trade. An increased balance of payments deficit on capital account would in any case be less serious if it were the experience of most of the industrialised countries; the pattern of receipts of foreign capital would be less likely to alter, since no one country would appear in an exceptionally unfavourable light to foreign investors.

The fact that all the industrialised countries would find themselves in an uncertain balance of payments position at the same time should improve the prospects for international co-operation over monetary problems. It might be possible to obtain agreement on rules for exchange rate variations and on increased liquidity through the International Monetary Fund, and it might also be possible to agree that all countries should make increased contributions to aid in an untied form. In that case increased foreign aid following upon disarmament would result in much larger potential export markets for all the industrialised countries.

Chapter 16

The Redistribution of
Defence Expenditure to Investment

Increases in investment are a major means of providing replacement expenditure on goods and services in the event of disarmament. The effects of increased investment are, however, much less easy to predict than the effects of increases in consumer income or government current spending, and there is also an appreciable time-lag before they can be felt. By adopting a cheap money policy in the years immediately following disarmament it might be possible for a government to stimulate a general increase in investment expenditure without itself using any of the funds released by disarmament for this purpose. A greater measure of control over the creation of the necessary replacement demand would on the other hand be available if more direct action, at a cost to the exchequer, were taken to increase the volume of investment. As it would also be felt that disarmament provided an opportunity to spend on several outstanding items of social investment, it would be likely that in addition to the provision of cheap money and a general encouragement to industry and local government to invest, a number of specific investment programmes, both in the productive and the social categories, would be carried out.

PRODUCTIVE INVESTMENT

Private Investment. Government influence upon investment by private industry can be exercised both directly through grants or subsidies, and indirectly through tax reliefs. Total government grants and subsidies to private industry in 1961/62 amounted to £401 million, of which £284 million consisted of agricultural subsidies. The rest was distributed as shown in Table 83.

The greater part of this assistance can be classified as assistance for investment. It does not include government assistance for research, which will be covered in the next section.

TABLE 83 *Government Assistance to Private Industry, 1961/62*

£ million

6·0	Cotton industry reorganisation (scrapping and re-equipment)
8·0	Aircraft industry (help for civil development, proving and production)
30·0	Help to firms setting up in low employment districts
2·5	Export promotion and miscellaneous
30·0	Steel industry (loan to Colvilles)
40·0	Building society loans
0·5	Scottish fisheries
117·0	Total

In the two years immediately following disarmament, government grants and loans might be made available to certain industries and firms particularly badly affected, as was suggested in Chapter 12, on the lines of the assistance recently given to the cotton, aircraft and steel industries. It is unlikely, however, that this direct form of assistance would continue much beyond the period immediately after disarmament had taken place, with the possible exception of any increase in help to firms setting up in development areas.

The diversion of defence expenditure to private investment would be most likely to be carried out through the taxation system. The machinery for this already exists in the form of the initial and investment allowances for capital expenditure, both of which take the form of a percentage of the value of the newly purchased asset, which may be deducted from taxable income. Initial allowances apply to expenditure on industrial buildings, machinery and plant and mining works, and are granted in the year in which the expenditure is incurred; investment allowances apply to new industrial and agricultural buildings, machinery and plant, mining assets and expenditure on scientific research.

The rate of allowance varies between several different types of asset, and is frequently changed. Rates on the more important categories of asset in recent years are shown in Table 84. The value of initial and investment allowances to a company must however vary according to whether the company is in fact making a profit on which tax relief can be claimed; Table 84 also shows the value of total initial and investment

TABLE 84. *The Rates and Value of Initial and Investment Allowances, and Gross Fixed Capital Formation by Companies, 1954–1960*

	1954 from April	1955	1956 from Feb. 18	1957 from April 9	1958 from April 15	1959 from April 7	1960
Initial allowances (per cent):							
New industrial buildings	nil	nil	10	10	15	5	5
Motorcars, secondhand plant and ships	20	20	20	20	30	30	30
Other new plant and machinery	nil	nil	20	20	30	10	10
Investment allowances (per cent):							
New buildings	10	10	nil	nil	nil	10	10
Scientific research assets[1]	20	20	20	20	20	20	20
Ships	20	20	20	40	40	40	40
Other plant and machinery	20	20	nil	nil	nil	20	20
Total initial and investment allowances to private industry (£ million)[2]	173	223	249	288	263	406	443
Gross fixed capital formation by companies (£ million)[2]	782	964	1,184	1,356	1,413	1,453	1,647

[1] Scientific assets do not qualify for an initial allowance as such, but the annual allowance in the first year is increased from 20 to 60 per cent, and those in the next four years are reduced from 20 per cent to 10 per cent.

[2] Figures are for calendar years.

Sources: Report of Commissioners of Inland Revenue 1961
Cmnd. 1598 and National Income and Expenditure 1961.

allowances in recent years, and it can be seen that the value of allowances actually fell in 1958, although the rates of the main initial allowances were increased.

Provided that some profits are being made, increased allowances do tend to encourage investment, although it is not possible to measure the effect which any specific increase will produce. It is also difficult to measure the cost of a proposed increase to the exchequer. On the assumption that the allowances granted in 1960 would otherwise all have been taxed at the standard rate, the cost to the exchequer in that year was in the region of £172 million. If in the event of disarmament the rates of all allowances were doubled, the additional cost to the exchequer would again be larger or smaller according to the proportions in which company profits had changed since 1960.

It is clear that companies making the largest profits would derive the most benefit from these measures. Increased investment by these companies would, however, have a multiplier effect upon the economy as a whole, while it is unlikely that any government would feel able to give direct support to unprofitable private companies for more than a very limited period after disarmament had taken place.

Nationalised Industries. Total investment by the nationalised industries and public corporations fell slightly in 1960/61 to a total of £865 million. This nevertheless amounted to over 20 per cent of gross fixed capital formation in that year, and 1961/62 and 1962/63 are expected to show a continued upward trend.

In the event of disarmament a general directive could be given to the nationalised industries to enlarge or accelerate their investment programmes. The extent to which this could be achieved without direct cost to the exchequer would vary, since there are considerable differences in the degree to which nationalised industries finance their own investment or draw upon the exchequer for investment capital. Total exchequer loans to the nationalised industries and public corporations in 1961/62 amounted to an estimated £555 million.[1] Expenditure by the Atomic Energy Authority is financed from a separate vote, and this amounted to £36 million, making a total of £591 million or of over 67 per cent of total estimated investment. Over the Electricity Council's seven year investment programme, however, only 52 per cent of capital is to be derived from exchequer loans, while exchequer contributions to investment by the National Coal Board, the Gas Council and the

---

[1] Interest receipts from previous loans amounted to £90 million in the same year, however, so that the net cost to the exchequer was £465 million.

TABLE 85 *Investment by the Nationalised Industries and Public Corporations*

1959/60 Actual prices	1960/61	1961/62 March, 1961	1962/63 prices	
Out-turn	Estimated out-turn	Forecast out-turn	Approved expenditure 1st October, 1961	
107·9	94·0	97·0	95·0	National Coal Board
47·6	43·3	47·0	48·8	Gas Council and Boards
317·8	297·7	324·5	355·5	Electricity Council and Boards
26·0	27·2	25·5	27·5	S. Scotland Electricity Board
13·4	11·1	12·8	13·5	N. Scotland Hydro-Electric Board
30·9	47·4	44·3	37·3	Air Corporations
206·0	204·0	175·0	177·2	British Transport Commission
37·3	35·7	36·1	32·4	Atomic Energy Authority
94·4	99·7	107·0	118·0	Post Office
5·1	5·6	11·8	10·0	Other
886·4	865·7	881·0	915·2	Total

Source: Cmnd. 1522 Public Investment in Great Britain, October, 1961.

Post Office in 1961/62 were in each case less than 40 per cent of the total. Investment by the Air Corporations and the British Transport Commission was, on the other hand, entirely covered by exchequer loans.

The only nationalised industries at present dealing with unsatisfied demand on a large scale are the electricity supply industry and the Post Office. Sales of electricity have been rising by an average 7 to 8 per cent over the last ten years, and increased still more sharply in 1961, although average consumption per head is still only about half of the American level. The electricity industry is already carrying out the largest single investment programme in the British economy, which involved the expenditure of £2,330 million between 1958 and 1965; this programme was increased in 1961 to cover an upward revision of the load forecast.

The current planned increase in generating capacity is already on so large a scale that it cannot be considered a priority for additional funds from defence expenditure, even though the industry is not receiving as much capital as it could usefully employ. The most serious deficiency in electricity capital programmes is in the reinforcement of the distribution system, which was estimated in 1962 to be some £100 million in arrears; if, as is probable, capital cannot be spared from investment in generating capacity in sufficient quantity to meet this need, it may still constitute a suitable outlet for defence funds for some years. The other main possible contribution from defence to investment in electricity would be if defence funds were used to increase the percentage of exchequer loans as against the 50 per cent of the investment programme which the industry currently plans to finance itself over the next five years; this could have the effect of enabling the investment programme to be carried out without further price increases. The decision to increase the dependence of any of the nationalised industries on exchequer financing is however a political rather than an economic question.

The United Kingdom is backward in telephone ownership in comparison with the United States, where there are 41 telephones per 100 inhabitants as compared to the British 16. There is a long waiting list for telephones, most of the delay being due to the lack of local cable installations. In 1961, however, the Post Office was freed from direct Treasury control, and its rate of expansion increased. A ten-year programme for the automatisation of the telephone service is to be completed by 1970, and investment in the telephone service has risen from £72·8 million in 1958/59 to an estimated £107·3 million in 1962/63. Although scope exists for a further increase in this investment programme, it seems probable that the greater part of demand will be met in any case from the existing sources of capital over the next few years.

One of the criteria for the diversion of defence funds to investment in the nationalised industries might be the tendency of the expansion of these industries to provide markets for types of products made by firms affected by disarmament, coupled with the existence of an unfulfilled demand in these sectors. The atomic energy programme, the railways and the airports were all mentioned by firms interviewed as possible alternative markets for products of the heavy and precision engineering, shipbuilding and electronics industries.

Investment by the Atomic Energy Authority has been maintained at a fairly steady level in recent years; its main production facilities were completed in 1960, and new investment now consists of a variety of smaller research and development projects. The main objective is still the development of nuclear reactors to generate electricity on an economic basis; the bulk of new investment from 1962 will be in development of the more advanced reactor systems for the next generation of nuclear power stations. The electricity industry's nuclear power programme was considerably slowed down in 1960, when economies of scale and improvements in manufacturing techniques had resulted in a large reduction in the cost of generating electricity by conventional means; present policy is to continue to build nuclear stations only on a scale adequate to maintain technological progress, which currently consists of placing orders for about one a year. Until nuclear power becomes competitive with other fuels, an increase in the nuclear power programme would be uneconomic. The only possible use for defence funds in this sector might be for increased spending on nuclear research, but this is already taking place on a large scale, and would in any case be likely to have been accelerated during the transition period through the transfer of resources from the military research programme.

Investment in the railways in 1961 amounted to £143 million, a fall of £30 million on the figure for 1959. Although there is still considerable scope for increased spending on the dieselisation and electrification of the railways, and this would provide a stimulant to the heavy and electrical engineering industries, uncertainty about the future of the railways is still too great for it to be possible to estimate the sort of sum which could usefully be diverted from defence for this purpose. The Transport Commission was also suggested as a possible market for shipbuilding firms; the largest amount spent on investment in ships in recent years was £4·3 million in 1959, so that even if this figure were doubled it would only amount to a moderate item of expenditure in comparison with total sales by the shipbuilding industry.

Expenditure by the two air corporations on aircraft and spares in 1961/62 was estimated at £34·7 million, and investment on premises, ground equipment, and office and commercial equipment was estimated at £9·6 million. Further expenditure on aircraft might be financed by the government in the event of disarmament in order to assist the aircraft industry, but this would bear little relation to present needs. A proportion of the corporations' expenditure on ground equipment, together with a sum in the region of £1 million which has been spent annually by the Ministry of Aviation in recent years on installations for airports, consists of investment in electronic and other equipment for air traffic control systems. There is considerable scope here for increased expenditure, which would provide a larger market for the electronics industry.

Research and Development. It has already been suggested[1] that in the two years following disarmament there would be a strong case for a high proportion of the government contribution to research and development for defence purposes to be transferred to research in the civil sector, largely in order not to waste valuable existing resources in the industries affected. This chapter, however, is concerned with the problem of increasing rather than maintaining investment after disarmament has taken place, and if total investment were to be increased, research and development should certainly be taken into account. Although expenditure on civil research doubled between 1955 and 1958, a more recent report[2] suggested that further research was urgently needed on the conservation of natural resources, in civil and electrical engineering, oceanography, astronomy and pure mathematics, as well as in many other fields, while many industries still need to build up a tradition of using the results of work which has already been carried out.

It was shown in Chapter 4 that expenditure on civil research and development amounted to some £243 million in 1958. Expenditure on research for defence purposes in 1960/61 was £240 million, so that if the whole of this sum were transferred to civil research expenditure it would increase its present value by an amount probably between 90 and 100 per cent. This would not in fact actually double the effort put into civil research, since defence research frequently has civil applications which are subsequently exploited.

There are several possible methods of increasing the total spent on research in the United Kingdom, but it seems most likely that a major change would only result from government expenditure. The investment allowance for expenditure on scientific assets is already very high (see note to Table 84), and it is doubtful whether to raise it further would have a significant influence on private industry's investment in research. It was recently estimated that the cost of increasing this investment allowance to 30 per cent would be in the region of £1·5 million a year; since the cost involved is a small one in comparison with the size of expenditure on defence, it would be worth making this change in case it did have an unexpectedly stimulating effect.

[1] Cf. p. 140–141.
[2] Advisory Council on Scientific Policy, 1959/60.

It would be of more importance, however, to increase government expenditure on civil research, and after the two year transition period were over a minimum of £100–150 million of the total previously spent for defence should continue to be provided for this purpose in order to prevent a major loss of stimulus to the economy. Government grants and loans to private industry could be given against a certain percentage contribution from the companies themselves, in order to encourage industrial spending, on the existing basis of grants to the research associations, but the government share would have to constitute a generous proportion.

Research and to some extent development could be carried out on an increased scale in government establishments, but the greater part of the additional expenditure on civil research could be channelled to private industry through the D.S.I.R. and N.R.D.C. The D.S.I.R. contribution to the co-operative research associations, now under £2 million, could be sharply increased. Research contracts for telecommunications in space, which would be an obvious alternative for research teams in aircraft and electronics during the interim period, could be continued indefinitely after the two years were up. Development contracts could be placed with the aircraft, electronics and machine tools industries, and wherever development costs are particularly heavy and technical advance of urgent importance. Research grants to the universities could also be considerably increased; the cost of work carried out by the universities[1] in 1958/59 at £23 million was only just over 8 per cent of the total expenditure on research and development.

The expansion of civil research on this scale would depend on the availability of qualified scientists and technologists, but with the release of some 10,000 of these from defence work and with the possibility of increased investment in education there should be no shortage.

SOCIAL INVESTMENT

Housing. The total stock of houses and flats in the United Kingdom at the end of 1961 is estimated at over 16·8 million, of which over 5 million are owner-occupied and over 4 million are owned by public authorities, the rest being privately rented. An appreciable proportion of this stock, however, consists of slum dwellings awaiting replacement, and there is a severe shortage in many places of rented accommodation.

---

[1] It may be noted that the United States National Science Foundation has predicted that investment in basic research in the American universities will increase by 200 per cent between 1962 and 1970.

In every year since 1959 more houses have been completed for private owners than for local housing authorities, but private owners seldom build to rent or build on sites which involve slum clearance.

TABLE 86 *Permanent Houses and Flats completed in the United Kingdom, 1958–1961*

thousands For local housing authorities	For private owners	Others	Total	
143·3	130·2	5·1	278·6	1958
124·5	153·2	3·9	281·6	1959
128·2	171·4	4·6	304·2	1960
116·1	180·7	6·3	303·2	1961

Source: Ministry of Housing and Local Government, Department of Health for Scotland and Ministry of Health, Northern Ireland.

Returns made by local authorities in 1955 indicated that there were then about 1 million slum dwellings which ought to be demolished; since each local authority used different definitions of what constituted a slum and since clearance programmes were limited to manageable proportions, this tended to underestimate actual requirements. It was shown in 1958[1] that out of 5 million privately rented houses and flats 2·8 million had no fixed bath, over 2·6 million had no hot water system and about 400,000 no flush lavatory, although in many cases these amenities could be installed in the existing houses. A more recent survey by the Ministry of Housing[2] showed that 3·75 million houses in England and Wales were built before 1880. A high estimate for the average life of a house is a hundred years, so it may be assumed that most of these will need replacement by 1980. At the same time estimates of the growth of households[3] suggest an average yearly increase of over 0·6 per cent between 1961 and 1980. On this basis an additional 2 million dwellings will have to be provided by 1980 for England and Wales alone.

Between January, 1956 and December, 1961, 360,000 slum dwellings were demolished and 1·8 million new houses and flats were built. Over the last three years an average of just over 60,000 slum dwellings have been demolished and just under 300,000 dwellings have been built in

[1] Rowntree Trust housing study.
[2] Cmnd. 1290, Housing in England and Wales. February 1961.
[3] L. Needleman—A long term view of housing. N.I.E.S.R. November, 1961.

each year. If 3 million slum houses were to be demolished by 1975 over 200,000 would have to be pulled down annually, and a similar number or a slightly larger one would have to be built in each year for replacement. At least 100,000 dwellings should be built in each year in order to keep pace with the formation of new households, making a total of over 300,000. This does not allow for the building of houses to satisfy other replacement demand arising from migration from a declining to an expanding area, or from the loss of houses to other types of development, nor does it make any provision for alleviating existing problems of overcrowding in houses which cannot be classified as slums, or for increased building for old people. It seems clear that to satisfy all these needs at least 350,000 houses and flats should be built annually. This would, however, also involve a change in the pattern of housebuilding; since the majority of households rehoused from slum dwellings would require rented accommodation and often at uneconomic rents, their demand would have to be met by the local housing authorities, who would consequently have to build at least 200,000 dwellings a year for this purpose alone. Total building by local authorities would probably amount in these circumstances to some 250,000, a figure which is 5,000 higher than the record for local authority building in 1953. Private building would be likely to be cut back to some extent, but unless it fell to 100,000 houses and flats a year, a reduction of over 40 per cent, the total number of dwellings completed annually would be in the region of 400,000. The largest total achieved so far has been 354,000 in 1954.

Although this increase seems a large one, the completion of 400,000 instead of 300,000 houses and flats a year would still leave the United Kingdom with a comparatively low rate of house building.

TABLE 87 *Comparative Rates of House Construction in Europe 1958–1960*

Dwellings completed
per 1,000 inhabitants

10·2	West Germany
9·0	Sweden
7·6	Netherlands
7·5	Norway
6·8	France
5·6	United Kingdom

Source: 'Housing and Economic Development' E.C.E. 1961.

Local authority building is financed mainly by borrowing, subject to the issue of loan sanction by the Minister of Housing or the Secretary of State for Scotland. Approved building by local authorities also attracts exchequer subsidies; these take the form of fixed annual payments in respect of each house completed, and have amounted in recent years to 23 per cent of the total annual charges, including maintenance and loan charges, on local authority buildings in England and Wales, and to 33 per cent in Scotland. Local authority building is also subsidised, to a much smaller extent, from rates. Building by the new town development corporations and the Scottish Special Housing Association, which are included in Table 86 under 'local housing authorities', is financed directly by loans repayable over 60 years from the exchequer.

Total public capital expenditure on housing is shown in Table 88.

TABLE 88 *Public Capital Expenditure on Housing in Great Britain*

1959/60	1960/61	1961/62[1]	1962/63[1]	
245·0	237·0	230·0	230·0	England and Wales
41·5	43·0	43·0	42·0	Scotland
286·5	280·0	273·0	272·0	Total

[1] Estimate
Source: Cmnd. 1522. Public investment in Great Britain, October 1961.

This table includes spending by local authorities, new town development corporations and housing associations on new building, the acquisition of land and buildings, and improvements. It does not exactly correspond with building 'for local housing authorities' in Table 86, which includes building in Northern Ireland and excludes building by housing associations, but neither of these items is large.

The total of the annual central government subsidies towards the cost of local authority building in England and Wales reached nearly £70 million in 1960/61. Government contributions towards conversion and improvements to existing houses amounted to £2·8 million. Government loans to the twelve new town development corporations increased by £18 million during 1961, reaching a total of £247 million. The remaining item of government finance for housing consisted of the loan to building societies for the finance of purchases of houses built before 1919. Although these houses constitute nearly half of the total stock, the building societies themselves are unwilling to lend for this purpose. The government loan amounted to £40 million in 1961/62, after which the scheme was suspended as part of the general measures to restrict public expenditure. During 1961, however, one new source of government finance was made available, consisting of loans up to a total of £25 million for non-profit-making housing associations building houses to let at economic rents.

In order to increase local authority building to 250,000 houses a year, public investment in housing would have to increase by over £280 million at the current rates. Since the cost of local authority building has been rising extremely rapidly (by 12·5 per cent in 1961), the amount would be likely to be appreciably higher. The total annual subsidies would on the basis of the present system also increase by some £70 million. The renewal of the government loan to building societies for the purchase of old houses is also considered an urgent priority, so that the total increase in public expenditure on housing if all these objects were to be achieved would be in the region of £400 million a year, consisting of nearly a third of total resources released by disarmament. According to the present system of housing finance, however, the greater part of this amount would normally be derived from private borrowing by the local authorities. Provided that private finance were available on this scale, the actual cost to the exchequer would be the increased annual subsidy towards loan charges and maintenance, and the expenditure of £70 million by the government would in that case be the means of stimulating total investment to the extent of four times that amount. Together with the renewed loan to the building societies, the total annual cost to the exchequer of the accelerated housing programme would amount to some £110 million.

It would be more likely, however, that so large an increase in local authority debt would have to be met to some extent from central funds. Advances from the Public Works Loan Board since 1958 have been confined to those local authorities who meet with 'real difficulty' in raising sufficient money from the mortgage or stock market, with the result that they were sharply reduced from a peak of over £340 million in 1954/55 to £36 million in 1958/59. Many local authorities might find difficulty in increasing their borrowing by more than 100 per cent, so that P.W.L.B. funds would have to be made available to them.

The total annual cost to the exchequer of an increase in local authority building to 250,000 houses a year, together with the renewal of the loan to building societies, would therefore lie between £110 million and £400 million, according to the method of finance used, although the total new annual investment would amount in any case to £400 million.

Education. Public investment in education has risen from £91 million in 1955/56 to an estimated £160 million in 1961/62. Capital expenditure on schools, further education and training colleges is made by the local education authorities; it is mostly financed by borrowing, and the loan charges together with capital expenditure from revenue are taken into account in calculating the general grant paid to local authorities by the exchequer. Capital expenditure by the universities is financed partly by themselves but mainly by the exchequer; a limit to the total value of the exchequer grant is fixed each year, and the University Grants Committee makes allocations within this sum between the various universities.

TABLE 89 *Public Investment in Education, 1961/62*

£ million

	England and Wales:
51·3	Primary and secondary schools
16·1	Further education
26·1	Other (including training colleges)
23·2	Land, plant, equipment, fees etc.
	Scotland:
11·8	Schools
5·7	Other
25·3	University Grants Committee

159·5

Source: Cmnd. 1522. Public Investment in Great Britain. October 1961.

School building. The largest single item of capital expenditure is on school building. A five year programme to build new schools and improve existing ones began in 1960/61; the total cost is estimated at £365 million, and work worth some £150 million had been started by the end of 1961/62. In January, 1961 the primary and secondary school population in England and Wales was 6·9 million, an increase of over 37,000 on the previous year. At the end of 1961 3 million children were in places provided since 1946, but just under half of the school population attended schools built before the 1914/18 war.

During the last half of 1960 the average building cost per new primary school place was £157·8, while the average cost per secondary school place was £282·4. If an average cost of £250 is assumed for all places, which allows for some rise in prices, the total cost of providing 3 million new school places would be in the region of £750 million a year. The current five year plan already allows for the spending of £365 million, so that a further £385 million could usefully be diverted from defence to school building if disarmament were to take place before 1965/66. Distributed over another five year plan this would amount to over £70 million a year. It may be assumed, however, that school building will continue at an annual level of at least £50 million after 1965/66, and this amount could be subtracted from the total needed from defence in each year after that date.

Teacher training. At the beginning of 1961 over 85,000 children aged over 11 were in 'all age' schools. Over 37 per cent of all children were in oversize classes (over 40 in a primary school and 30 in a secondary school); this proportion had fallen from 38·5 per cent a year earlier, but a further deterioration is expected in 1962/63, when the effects will be felt of the introduction of the three year course in the general training colleges in 1960.

Capital investment in the training colleges averaged about £1 million a year during the 1950's. In 1959 plans were made to provide an additional 24,000 training college places by 1966, involving expenditure of some £40 million. This programme will double the existing capacity of the training colleges, and it was believed in 1959 that it would result in the elimination of oversize classes by 1970. It has now been realised, however, that this plan was based on underestimates both of the birth rate and of the wastage rate of women teachers who marry and have children. A more realistic estimate[1] suggests that the average annual rate of recruitment of full-time teachers would have to be between 30,000 and 35,000 in each year of the 1960's in order to keep pace with the birth-rate and the voluntary demand to stay on at school after 15, to staff the expansion of the training colleges, and to eliminate oversize classes by 1970. The actual recruitment of full-time teachers in 1960/61 was 24,700. An additional 4,000 teachers will emerge from the training colleges in each year after 1965, and a further 4,000 a year by 1969; the situation may be improved if the number of part-time teachers continues to increase and the campaign to attract married women back to teaching meets with further success, but it is plain that oversize classes will in fact continue well into the 1970's.

[1] By John Vaizey and Simon Pratt: 'Investment for National Survival' National Union of Teachers, 1959.

Large additional numbers of teachers will also be needed in order to achieve reforms beyond these basic aims. It has been estimated[1] that in order to raise the school leaving age to 16, and to provide compulsory education on two days a week for children not at school aged between 16 and 18, about 20,000 extra teachers would be required if this took place in 1970. The reduction of primary classes to a maximum of 30 in the course of the 1970's would require at least another 50,000 teachers, and many more if the birth rate continues to rise.

The achievement of these reforms as well as of the current basic aims which were laid down in 1944 would bring the total teaching force in state primary and secondary schools, independent schools, colleges of further education and training colleges to an estimated minimum of 500,000. The total at the beginning of 1961 was in the region of 343,000, the net increase during 1960 having amounted to some 8,000.

The provision of additional permanent training college capacity is an extremely protracted method of obtaining more teachers, as seven years elapse while plans are approved, a college is built and the first three year course completed. According to existing plans, moreover, annual recruitment is likely to exceed 32,000 in any case by 1970; it has been suggested[2] that the average annual wastage rate of the total teaching force should be taken as 5·5 per cent, and on this basis annual recruitment, once the figure of 500,000 has been achieved, should be some 27,500. It might therefore appear that the best use of defence revenue for 'capital expenditure' on teacher training would be in financing a temporary training scheme for a more rapid provision of a number of additional teachers. This number would vary with the date at which defence revenue became available, and with trends in the birth rate and of the teacher wastage rate in future years. Existing buildings could be leased for this purpose, reducing the time taken to produce additional teachers by up to four years. The average cost of tuition and board in a general training college in 1959/60 was £438 per student; in a temporary scheme this might be increased to £600 to cover the cost of rent, equipment and a personal grant, making a total of £1,800 per student for a three-year course. This would be less if a proportion of the training facilities consisted of day training courses for older students, in particular married women, who constitute an important source for possible additional teachers. Personal grants for older students with dependents would, however, be higher.

[1] Vaizey and Pratt op. cit.
[2] Vaizey and Pratt op. cit.

The total cost of a temporary training scheme for 100,000 students would on the basis of these assumptions be in the region of £180 million, or £60 million a year if it were possible for all students to embark on the course simultaneously. The annual cost would in fact be appreciably less, as the availability of training college staff and of suitable students would make it necessary to spread a scheme on this scale over more than three years.

Universities. The annual cost to the exchequer of university building has risen from £7·5 million in 1951/52 to £25·3 million in 1961/62. The number of full-time students has meanwhile risen from 84,000 to 111,000.

The United Kingdom compares unfavourably with other countries in the provision of places in higher education as a whole. An O.E.C.D. survey published in 1961 showed that out of 19 member countries in 1958/59 the United Kingdom had almost the lowest percentage of the 20–24 age group in universities, teacher training colleges and comparable institutions of higher education. Although progress has been made since 1958/59, other countries have also been expanding their facilities.

TABLE 90 *Total National Students in Relation to Population Aged 20–24, 1958–1959*

per cent	Ranking order for 19 O.E.C.D. countries	
29·2	1	United States
7·7	2	Canada
7·3	3	Belgium
6·9	5	France
3·5	15	Germany
2·8	18	United Kingdom

Source: Policy Conference on Economic Growth and Investment in Education: V. International Flows of Students. O.E.C.D. 1961

Applications for entrance to British universities in 1961 amounted to 190,000, while the total admitted was 25,000. Since the majority of students apply to more than one university, the real total of applications is much less, but it is nevertheless true that there are far more school leavers both qualified and anxious to go to a university than there are places open to them. In recent years the main cause of the widening gap between applicants and places has been the trend for a growing proportion of students to stay on at school after reaching 17, which has itself been fostered by rising incomes and by more liberal government awards to students. After 1961, however, this trend will be accentuated by the effects of the increase in the birth rate in the middle 1940's.

Estimates made by the University Grants Committee in 1957 suggested that university places should be increased to an outside limit of 135,000 by 1965. Revised estimates made in 1959 showed that the number of places needed would be closer to 175,000 by the early 1970's. On this basis the exchequer non-recurrent grant was increased from £20·4 million in 1960/61 to £25 million in 1961/62; a further £25 million was promised for 1962/63 and £30 million in each of the next two years, and authority was given in 1960 and 1961 for the establishment of six more universities.

No plans have yet been announced for spending on university building after 1965, but past trends indicate that, unless there is a sharp rise in prices, expenditure of about £30 million a year from 1966 to 1971 would provide the necessary buildings and equipment, although without improvement on the present standards, for 175,000 students by 1973/74. This would represent a 75 per cent increase on the number of university students in 1959. An increase of more than 175 per cent would be necessary in the numbers of students in higher education as a whole in order to achieve the Canadian level in 1959. The general training colleges are to increase their capacity by 100 per cent and the colleges of advanced technology by nearly 300 per cent by the early 1970's, but these two sectors of higher education only accounted for some 12 per cent of total students in 1959. It may be argued that the main expansions in higher education should take place in the training colleges and the regional and other colleges outside the universities, but a university expansion of at least 100 per cent on 1959 seems a minimum requirement. This would add some £10 million a year to building costs.

In addition to this increase in spending, a contribution from defence sources could be made towards speeding up the university expansion programme. The spending of £70 million a year after 1964 instead of £40 million would enable the programme to be completed by 1970. The total contribution from defence would in that case amount to £40 million a year.

None of these figures for capital expenditure on the universities allow for the increased costs of awards to students, although these may equally well be regarded as an investment. Grants to all students in higher education reached £51·5 million in 1960/61, and these will increase at least in proportion to the additional percentage of places provided.

Road Building. In 1957 the costs of road congestion were estimated at £170 million a year, exclusive of loss of working time, and at £500 million if working time was included. Public investment in roads has not kept pace with private investment in vehicles, and although government spending has increased sharply in recent years the problems of congestion are still far from being solved. Total investment in new roads from exchequer funds is expected to be £90·5 million in 1962/63, an increase of 33 per cent on expenditure in 1959/60. The total exchequer contribution to the 1962–67 road building programme for England and Wales is estimated at £540 million; together with the contribution for Scotland and local authority expenditure from rates, total investment in roads is expected to average some £150 million a year by the mid-1960's. Meanwhile the number of vehicles on the roads is expected to increase from 8·5 million in 1959 to 14 million in 1966.

These investment plans are on a smaller scale than is considered sufficient by many road users. The British Road Federation has recently suggested a figure of £180 million to £200 million a year for five years; the Federation of Civil Engineering Contractors estimated in 1960 that investment could be increased from £75 million to £175 million a year without straining the industry's capacity, since nearly half the road-making plant owned by major contractors was at that time lying idle. The extra labour necessary for an increase of that size was estimated at 33,000.

It has also been pointed out that two-thirds of the investment planned under the five year programme is destined for the major trunk routes, so that only £50 million a year will be available for relieving urban congestion. It is often suggested, however, that urban problems will be solved in the long run by restrictive measures and by subsidised public transport, rather than exclusively by new roads.

It seems probable that investment in roads could usefully be increased by at least another £50 million a year for five years. On the basis of the 1960 estimate, this would involve the employment of an additional 16,500, largely unskilled, men on road building. A large proportion of this sum would probably go to urban road building schemes; if it were spent on motorways, however, assuming that costs were similar to those estimated for 1962, it would pay for the construction of some 70 miles.

HospitalBuilding. A large proportion of the hospital buildings taken over by the National Health Service in 1948 were in strikingly bad condition, 45 per cent having been built before 1900. The N.H.S. was however kept short of capital for many years, and no new hospital was started till 1954. Even between 1954 and 1958 the proportion of national income allotted to hospital building was still half of that achieved in 1938.

Annual expenditure on hospital building has now risen from £10·6 million in 1955/56 to £31 million in 1961/62, and at the beginning of 1962 a new ten-year hospital building programme was announced. This programme includes the building of 110 new hospitals in England and Wales, and major additions and improvements to some 500 existing hospitals. All projects are to be started by 1972. Expenditure on new hospitals over this period will amount to £500 million, and expenditure on improvements to £200 million; a further £95 million may be added to these figures for expenditure in Scotland, making a total of £795 million.

This figure is believed to be not much lower than that requested by the hospital boards, and it is similar to the £750 million which was suggested in 1959 by a committee of the British Medical Association as the sum necessary to be spent over ten years in order to modernize the hospital system. Since projects need not be completed until 1975, however, this amount will be distributed over thirteen years rather than ten[1], and no fixed annual amount has been laid down. The programme is to be reviewed annually, so that a ten year plan will always be in existence, and each year's expenditure will depend upon the state of the economy and of the building industry, although at its peak hospital building is not expected to take more than 4 per cent of constructional output. The main deficiency of the programme seems to be the possibility that much expenditure may be delayed until the end of the ten years is in sight.

If expenditure is distributed over thirteen years, the annual amount will average £61 million, or not quite double the expenditure in 1961/62. Released defence expenditure could be used to make this a genuine ten-year programme, in which case the annual expenditure would average £79 million, an increase of £18 million a year or of £180 million over the ten years. The existence of the annual review procedure would facilitate the adjustment of the programme in the event of disarmament.

[1] The Scottish plan is in fact a genuine ten year programme for the expenditure of £70 million. The Scottish figure for the next thirteen years has been used here for purposes of comparison.

Chapter 17

The Relationship between
Replacement Expenditure and Revenue

In Chapters 14 to 16 different ways of spending the resources which would be released in the event of disarmament have been examined, and estimates have been given both of the total expenditure which would be generated in each case and of the likely cost to the revenue of implementing each particular project. It was seen in Chapter 13 that these two need not necessarily coincide, and it should be stressed that it is the need to maintain expenditure which is of paramount importance; revenue considerations are of a secondary nature. On one set of assumptions, for example, the extra expenditure required might be generated at a cost to the revenue of only £1,000 million, leaving £500 million free to be used for other purposes. It is possible, on the other hand, to envisage a scheme of expenditure which would require the use of £2,000 million of revenue, and in this instance the extra revenue would have to be found either from the budget surplus or by deficit spending (or by a combination of both).

The extent to which revenue outpayments differ from the expenditure generated will depend upon the type of expenditure concerned and the means used to stimulate it. In the case of consumers' expenditure, if the increase were to be generated by cuts in the standard rates of income tax, the current high marginal propensity to save would make it necessary to release a total of some £710 million in order to obtain an extra £500 million of expenditure. This estimate does not take account of the fact that a large proportion of the tax cut would accrue to companies, and there is no way of assessing how much of this would in fact go to shareholders in the form of increased dividends. Other methods of reducing income tax, such as increasing personal allowances or the earned income allowance, would not be subject to this reservation, although it is still probable that a significant proportion of the extra income would be saved rather than spent, so that the cost to the revenue would be greater than the increase in expenditure required.

Reductions in the rates of purchase tax are more likely to raise expenditure by broadly the same amount as the cost to the revenue, although it would not be possible to estimate their results with complete accuracy, and they could well generate more expenditure than the loss of revenue involved. It is possible to be more dogmatic about the effect of giving increased income to the needy in the form of, for example, old age pensions or national assistance, since it is reasonable to assume that nearly all the extra income would, in fact, be spent.

Similarly, the cost to the revenue of increasing public authorities' current expenditure on goods and services by £250 million would, in the first instance, be equal to the extra expenditure concerned. Much of this extra expenditure is however likely to take the form of higher wages and salaries to government employees, so that part of it would return in the form of both direct and indirect taxes. In the case of aid to underdeveloped countries, the method of distribution adopted would in part determine how much of the extra £250 million would be spent in the United Kingdom. In the case of tied aid all of the money would, in theory at least, be spent in this country, but there could be a substitution effect which would be reflected in a fall in other exports to the country or countries concerned. If the recipient countries were left free to dispose of the aid as they saw fit, the value of orders placed in the United Kingdom would depend on the competitiveness of British industry and on such factors as credit or payment terms. It was pointed out in Chapter 15 that there is a considerable range of possibilities in the field of aid and that a number of uncertainties would be involved which could only be resolved by experience. To this extent, therefore, it is not possible to assess the cost to the revenue of obtaining a specified increase in exports as a result of increasing foreign aid.

Finally, there is considerable uncertainty about the cost to the revenue of increasing investment by a set amount of £500 million. In the conditions prevailing at the time of general disarmament it would theoretically be possible, and desirable, to induce investment by means of a 'cheap money' policy, which would not involve the use of the former defence revenue at all. The use of investment allowances to increase private industrial and commercial capital expenditure would also increase investment by more than their cost to the revenue (providing that they were of less than 100 per cent), although it is not possible to determine just how much extra investment they would, in fact, stimulate. There is less uncertainty about the amount of investment that could be induced in the public sector, but here again there is still considerable scope for different methods of financing to be adopted. In the case of housebuilding, for example, it was seen in Chapter 16 that the cost to the exchequer of raising local authority building from 116,000 to 250,000 houses a year would lie between £110 million and £400 million according to the method of financing selected, although, whatever the method, expenditure would total £400 million.

Since it is impossible to predict with accuracy the cost to the revenue of replacing £1,500 million of defence expenditure with the same amount of non-defence spending, it would be unwise to expect that any surplus revenue would become available, and the possibility that a greater sum would have to be spent must not be ignored. If the revenue required were less than £1,500 million the surplus could be used for other purposes. The uses to which it might be put are, of course, very wide and the choice would lie with the government of the day. In these circumstances, however, once the extra expenditure had been safely generated, it would be possible to use any spare revenue to reduce the national debt, an objective sometimes put forward as a suitable use for the resources likely to be released in the event of disarmament.

The national debt now totals over £28,000 million, (in nominal values), so that even if the whole annual saving on defence expenditure were devoted to its reduction, it would be nearly twenty years before the capital were paid off, exclusive of the interest payments made over this time. The annual cost in interest payments is very high; in 1961/62 this was effectively £935 million, although interest receipts amounting to £325 million from Government loans to local authorities and nationalized industries are deducted from this to give the above-the-line figure. Real interest payments have increased by nearly 90 per cent over the last ten years, largely as a result of a dear money policy, although the debt itself has only increased by some 10 per cent.

Although a reduction in the annual cost of interest payments would be a useful saving, the amount of capital repayment necessary to make any appreciable effect on these is extremely large. The average interest paid is just over 3·5 per cent on nominal values, so that the reduction of the debt by £500 million a year, or by one-third of defence expenditure, would result in a reduction in interest payments of £18 million[1] a year,

---

[1] This would vary with the type of government security bought back. Many would be obtainable at less than their nominal value, so that the reduction in interest payments could be rather larger.

or by 1·8 per cent. In exchange for a very small saving in interest payments, large sums of capital would be transferred from revenue used to pay for defence expenditure to the savings deposits or the safe, fixed interest investments of the cautious investor. It is unlikely that more than a very small proportion of the repaid debt would find its way back to productive investment, so that the general effect of repayments of the national debt would be to hold back capital formation and spending instead of encouraging their growth.

Appendix A

Garrison Towns and Defence Expenditure

In an attempt to discover how individual garrison towns might be affected in the event of disarmament, studies were carried out in two such towns—Aldershot and Chatham. These studies consisted mainly of interviews with persons concerned with the administration of the towns and with local industry and commerce, and additional information about the numbers of civilians employed by the services was obtained from the Admiralty and the War Office.

A brief summary of the results was given in Part I, page 12, and the most important conclusion to be drawn from them was that the wide differences between the two towns and their nearby regions made it impossible to generalise about the prospects for garrison towns as a whole. Each one will clearly have to be considered individually, both in the light of the general employment situation in the area and the dependence of local manufacturing industry on defence contracts.

1. *Aldershot*

The town of Aldershot, and the Aldershot and Farnborough area as a whole, has enjoyed growing prosperity in recent years. New light industries have entered the area, which also serves to a certain extent as a dormitory for workers in London, and the demand for labour has grown steadily. In January, 1962, unemployment at 0·6 per cent of the labour force was under half the national average, and it was reported that workers travelled daily from as far away as Portsmouth to work in the region.

Total employment in Aldershot and Farnborough was in the region of 29,000 workers, and some 5,000 of these were employed by the garrison and in army workshops. Neither the services nor the local industries were able to obtain all the labour they required, and the position was aggravated by the current Army rebuilding programme. This is expected to cost a total of £18 million, and in addition to the usual service facilities includes provisions for the building of a large number of modern married-quarters.

It is expected that a local field stores, employing about 600 civilians, is to be closed down in the course of the next year or two due to an Army reorganization scheme. It was considered typical of the current climate of opinion that when this was first announced the news did not even rate a prominent position in the local newspaper, though some of the persons interviewed could remember a time when such an event would have had severe repercussions on the entire town. In this instance, however, it is expected that the Army itself will be able to find alternative jobs for nearly all the workers involved, and that even if this were not the case they would easily be able to find civil employment.

In the face of this general feeling of confidence it is, perhaps, not surprising that the prospect of general disarmament was viewed with equanimity. To a certain extent this confidence derives from the knowledge of the current Army rebuilding programme, since it is felt that even if disarmament were to occur an alternative use would be found for the facilities available. In addition, there are the newly built married-quarters, and it was felt that if they were turned over to the local authority in the event of disarmament, it would help to solve the local housing shortage which is partly held responsible for the shortage of workers in the area.

No industry or firm in the area was thought to be dependent on defence expenditure to any great extent, either from the garrison or from defence contracts, though some companies were known to have defence contracts. Because of the well-equipped N.A.A.F.I. shop serving the soldiers and their families, the local shops were not thought to rely on service expenditure for a significant proportion of their sales. This was less true of the public houses, cinemas and cafes in the area, all of which were expected to suffer a significant reduction in trade if the garrison were to close down—in the short term at least. These were the exception, however, and they were not considered to be of sufficient importance to have a marked effect on the economy of the area as a whole, which was expected to grow whether disarmament did, or did not, occur.

2. Chatham

People were considerably more reluctant to discuss the probable effect on the region of disarmament in the Chatham area than was the case in Aldershot. One informant said that this reluctance reflected the concern in the town about the possibility of any change in the level of employment at the Naval dockyard and, to a lesser extent, at the nearby School of Military Engineering. Unemployment in the area, which includes Gillingham, Rochester and Strood as well as Chatham, stood at 2·5 per cent of the labour force at the beginning of 1962. The working population of the area, excluding those employed at Service establishments and in the dockyards, totalled nearly 67,000 in June, 1960, the latest period for which figures were available, and is not thought to have changed to any great extent since that date. Admiralty employees in the area, both at the dockyards and other minor establishments, stood at 11,652 at January 1, 1962, of whom, 1,806 were non-industrial workers, 3,923 were skilled industrial workers, 4,876 were semi- and unskilled industrial workers and 1,047 were apprentices. Employment by the Army, mainly at the School of Military Engineering, totalled 949 persons, of whom 271 were non-industrial workers, 271 were skilled industrial workers and 407 were semi- and non-skilled industrial workers.

Chatham, despite its long connection with the Navy, is no longer a garrison town of importance, and it is the dockyard which provides the majority of the employment in the area which is related to defence expenditure. The town has already suffered as a result of the closing of the nearby dockyard at Sheerness, when a number of the displaced workers tried to find similar work in Chatham. Though a high proportion of the workers concerned are skilled or semi-skilled, they are said to have difficulty in adapting themselves to other kinds of work.

A number of new industries and firms have been established in the area, but they are not large employers of labour, and in a number of instances employ mainly females. The dockyards, however, remain the largest single employer by a wide margin, and if they were to be closed down it was felt that the town of Chatham in particular, and the neighbouring towns to a lesser extent, would suffer a severe setback. Gillingham would be most affected by the closing of Army establishments.

Under the present conditions it was considered unlikely that more than a small proportion of the displaced workers would be able to find alternative employment in the area, and that, as a result, the local traders would experience a sharp reduction in their sales. The people interviewed were, however, either unwilling or unable to suggest suitable measures to counter the depression that was expected to result if disarmament were to take place, except to point out that they felt it would be the responsibility of the government to deal with the situation. Given the high level of defence-based employment in the area and this prevailing attitude, it seems clear that disarmament could well have an adverse effect on the Chatham area, at least if adequate steps were not taken to provide suitable alternative employment and to retain the workers concerned well before defence expenditure ceased.

Appendix B

A copy is given below of the questionnaire sent to the companies known or believed to carry out defence work. The analysis of the replies is given in Part I, Chapter 3, Defence Expenditure and the Firm, page 18.

DISARMAMENT ENQUIRY

CONFIDENTIAL

Name of company ....

Industry or business in which engaged ....

Total number of employees ....

1. What proportion of your company's total turnover represents defence contracts?

    10 per cent and under ....

    11 to 25 per cent   ....

    26 to 50 per cent   ....

    51 to 75 per cent   ....

    76 to 100 per cent   ....

2. How many employees are wholly (or mostly) engaged on defence work?   ....

3. In which of the following standard regions of the country is this work carried out?

    Northern   .... South Western   ....

    E. & W. Riding .... Wales   ....

North Midland	Midland ....
Eastern	North Western ....
London & S.E.	Scotland ....
Southern	N. Ireland ....

4. Please indicate the main scope of the defence work undertaken, e.g. manufacture of aircraft, aircraft equipment, armaments, weapons, electronic equipment, army clothing, vehicles etc.

   ....

   ....

5. What proportion of your company's research expenditure is financed by defence contracts?

10 per cent and under	....
11 to 25 per cent	....
26 to 50 per cent	....
51 to 75 per cent	....
76 to 100 per cent	....

6. How far do you estimate that the resources currently engaged on defence contracts could readily be transferred to non-defence purposes?

   ....

   ....

7. What do you feel are the main problems likely to face your company in the event of the complete cessation of defence contracts?

   ....

   ....

   ....

   ....

A copy of the following letter was sent with the questionnaire, addressed to the managing director of the company concerned:

Dear Sir,

The Economist Intelligence Unit Limited has been commissioned by the United World Trust for education and research to carry out an objective study of the likely economic consequences of disarmament in the United Kingdom. The Trust undertakes activities of an educational and research nature and is recognised as a charitable organization for taxation purposes. It is not, therefore, able to propagate a particular individual's or organization's viewpoint, and this ensures that the survey will be of a purely objective nature.

All responsible persons, of whatsoever political persuasion, realise that defence expenditure accounting for some 7 per cent of the Gross National Product is an important factor in our economic life, and that any significant alteration in its level would have marked repercussions on the economy as a whole. One major cause of concern, for example, is the fear that the ending of defence contracts would lead to large-scale unemployment. For this reason, a factual study of the ways in which this expenditure affects different sectors of the economy should prove a valuable guide as to the nature of the problems likely to arise as a result of disarmament, as well as providing an indication of how they could best be resolved.

The enclosed questionnaire is designed to discover the importance of defence spending to U.K. industry, and we should be grateful for your co-operation in supplying the information required. No secret or technical information is involved, and the individual returns will be treated in the strictest confidence and only used to build up an overall picture of the industry or industries concerned. If your company is divided into a number of distinct operating divisions or groups which it would be easier to treat separately, we will be very pleased to send you extra copies of the questionnaire.

It is intended to follow up the questionnaire by a series of interviews with concerns that depend on defence contracts to any significant extent in order to obtain their views on the likely mobility of the resources involved and the difficulties which may well arise from their transfer to non-defence purposes in the event of a substantial measure of disarmament.

We trust you will feel able to co-operate with us in this enquiry into an extremely complex and important subject, and look forward to receiving your reply.

Yours faithfully,

Appendix C

The Estimated Cost to the Exchequer of implementing the Proposals considered in Chapters 14-16

Annual cost[1] on the basis of 1961 costs	
£ million	**1. To increase consumers' disposable income by 2·6 per cent on the 1961 total**
	By means of:—
	1. *Income tax relief*
100	An increase in the earned income allowance from $\frac{2}{9}$ to $\frac{1}{4}$
120	An increase in personal allowances from £140 to £160 (single) and £240 to £260 (married)
40	An increase of £20 in each of the children's allowances
16	Abolition of income tax on family allowances and small private pensions
	2. *Purchase tax relief*
86	Reduction of purchase tax to 25 per cent, on motor cars
26	on radios, television sets, gramophones, records
90	Reduction of purchase tax by at least half on clothing, furniture, floor coverings, domestic appliances
	2. To increase consumers' disposable income through the social services
100–125	To increase *old age pensions* from 57s. 6d. to 65s. (single) and from 92s. 6d. to 105s. (married)
41–48	To increase *other flat rate national insurance benefits* by similar amounts, together with increases for dependents
13	To increase *national assistance* scale rates from 57s. 6d. to 65s. (single) and from 95s. 6d. to 108s. (married), together with increases for dependents
33	To increase *family allowances* from 8s. to 10s. for the second child and from 10s. to 12s. 6d. for subsequent children

[1] All these figures are rough estimates. The costs shown in Section I, in particular, are liable to increase in every year after 1961 in which there is an increase in national income.

3. To increase government current expenditure at home and abroad

1. By raising the wages and salaries of government employees

52   *Teachers*—to implement the N.U.T. proposal for 1961

30–40[1]   *Nurses*—to implement the 1961 pay claim

40   Others

2. By increased aid to developing countries

150–255   To increase aid from Britain by 50 to 85 per cent on the total for 1961

4. To increase investment[2]

1. Productive investment

172[3]   *Private industry:* to double the rates of investment and initial allowances

100   *Nationalized industries:* reinforcement of the electricity distribution system

n.a.   Post office, air corporations, railways

1·5   *Research and development:* to increase the investment allowance to 30 per cent

100–150   Government grants and loans to industry and the universities, and expenditure in government establishments

2. Social investment

110–400[4]   *Housing:* to increase local authority building from 116,000 to 250,000 houses a year

77   *Education:* to build 308,000 extra new school places a year for 5 years

30   to finance a temporary 6 year training scheme to train 100,000 extra teachers

38   to enlarge the university expansion scheme from a 75 per cent increase between 1959 and 1973 to 100 per cent between 1959 and 1970

50   *Roads:* to increase the 1962–67 road building programme from £150 million to £200 million a year

18   *Hospitals:* to complete the hospital building programme by 1972 instead of 1975

[1] The September 1962 award now makes the lower figure more realistic.

[2] The investment programmes suggested for electricity distribution, school building and roads would be spread over not more than five years while the other items of social investment also have a time limit.

[3] This figure would show great variation with the state of company profits.

[4] According to the method of financing chosen.

Tables

218

220

Index

Lightning Source UK Ltd.
Milton Keynes UK
UKHW012357200722
406167UK00001B/336